The Philosophy of Labour

C. Delisle Burns

RFF PRESS
RESOURCES FOR THE FUTURE

First published in 1925
by George Allen and Unwin Ltd.

This edition first published in 2016 by Routledge
2 Park Square, Milton Park, Abingdon, Oxon, OX14 4RN
and by Routledge
711 Third Avenue, New York, NY 10017

Routledge is an imprint of the Taylor & Francis Group, an informa business

Publisher's Note
The publisher has gone to great lengths to ensure the quality of this reprint but points out that some imperfections in the original copies may be apparent.

Disclaimer
The publisher has made every effort to trace copyright holders and welcomes correspondence from those they have been unable to contact.

A Library of Congress record exists under LC control number: 26005401

ISBN 13: 978-1-138-12254-3 (hbk)
ISBN 13: 978-1-315-65043-2 (ebk)
ISBN 13: 978-1-138-12255-0 (pbk)

Routledge Revivals

The Philosophy of Labour

Originally published in 1925, C. Delisle Burns' *The Philosophy of Labour* attempts to lay down key aspects of labour and the working class of that time period, covering aspects such as economic obstacles, standards of living and patriotism. Burns does not draw on past philosophers or sociological thinkers of the working-class and instead chose to focus only on the attitude of the workers in factories, mines, roads, railways and other forms of manual labour. This title will be of interest to students of philosophy.

THE PHILOSOPHY OF LABOUR . .

THE PHILOSOPHY OF LABOUR

BY

C. DELISLE BURNS

LONDON: GEORGE ALLEN & UNWIN LTD.
RUSKIN HOUSE, 40 MUSEUM STREET, W.C. 1

First published in 1925

Printed in Great Britain by
UNWIN BROTHERS, LIMITED, LONDON AND WOKING.

To

MY FRIENDS

AMONG THE RAILWAYMEN, THE MINERS,
THE COTTON-SPINNERS, THE POST-OFFICE
WORKERS, AND THE TEACHERS IN
ELEMENTARY SCHOOLS

PREFACE

This is what I have learnt—not from books. It is a statement of the point of view of manual workers. I do not overestimate the ability of my teachers, for their conceptions are not altogether clear; but I think this is what they mean. It is their contribution to the life of our time. Their point of view is significant, even if the number of workers who have acquired it is small. No programme or policy is discussed here: all I have attempted is a short statement of the attitude which arises from the experience of workers, and is the basis of their claims and their hopes. I trust that the readers of this book will not think of the doctrines of Marx or of Mill, but of the experience of workers in factories and mines, on roads and on railways.

C. DELISLE BURNS.

London,
July 1925.

CONTENTS

The Philosophy of Labour

I

CIVILIZATION

How has it happened that men no longer scratch the ground with flint implements? How has it happened that they fly and hear one another speak across a thousand miles? The answer can be found by understanding what is meant by Labour.

In Ancient Greece the temple standing in its grove of trees was the meeting-place for all the citizens. Their own hands had built it for their own pleasure in the common service of what they held to be divine. In the grove they sang and danced and played their games. They placed within and around the temple the best of their sculpture and painting, and its structure was based upon all the resources of their science. There, on appointed days, for many generations they sacrificed and worshipped in the sense of a common security won by effort out of chaos and barbarism. They rejoiced together because they felt that each depended upon the other for most of what made life worth living. Their temples were not a contradiction of their ordinary lives. The sense of unity in the group, expressed outwardly in ceremony, was never far below the surface of consciousness in their business or their pleasures; and therefore the greatest offences were held to be those which endangered the communal life. But the community did not include all who lived together, as it did not include the dogs or the plants. There were slaves—in poor cities few and in great cities an increasing number as wealth increased. Of doubtful status between that of the ruling men and the slaves, there were the free women of the city. Some held that women were defective as the slave who was actually slavish was defective in what distinguished humanity from the beast. But among the few free men there was a full sense of community, of equality, and of the dependence of each upon all. It was not an ideal world but, like all worlds, it had ideal elements in it; and these have survived in the glamour of the past. One could construct Utopia out of the elements of Greek civilization if history did not remind us of the fact that the Greeks themselves were not satisfied.

The great Roman world which absorbed the Greek arts, built its own community. As the temples stand for Greece, so the baths and villas and roads stand for Rome. Civilization had expanded by new labour and thought; although again there was much evil, for slavery grew worse. But the basic strength and the fine bodily life symbolized in the baths were greater than the barbarism which eventually overwhelmed them. The community made by Rome was wider, more varied and much more lasting than any Greek community. But that civilization collapsed, and the new barbarism hardly preserved the rags of that old glory.

A thousand years later, in the succession of events which has led to the appearance of our peculiar beliefs and habits, the people of small cities in Europe gathered again on appointed days at new buildings—the great churches of the Middle Ages. These too had been built by their own hands, in some cases at their own expense and in their own spare time, for a service common to all the inhabitants of the city. They looked together for another better world, for they were sensible of their common fortunes in this. Manual work had been given a dignity by the Christian tradition, for Christ had been a carpenter and his chief apostles had been manual workers. All men stood erect because all were children of God and in the churches all men were equal.

The mediæval church was not merely a place for worship or the contemplation of other worlds; it was the general meeting-place for hearing music, for seeing the latest sculpture and painting; and, unless the town had grown large, it was a place for making business contracts, for school, for the dance, and for drama. It was the common possession of all the citizens, for all had the same faith and followed the same fundamental customs. Again, the sense of common life, expressed in ceremony, was not far below the surface of consciousness in business or pleasure. Guild organization kept alive the ideal of service in trade and manufacture under the inspiration of religious enthusiasm; and folk-dances, folk-music and common holidays united all classes.

Mediævalism can become the basis for Utopia now because of the inspiring elements in the life of those times, but a candid historian must admit that the best men then looked for a different world. Poverty and dirt and suffering were widespread, tyranny frequent, ignorance general, and even the dominant religion intermittent in its operation and often pernicious in its effects. But that world is dead.

Our ancestors in Western Europe and in America were the men and women of the Middle Ages. We share the mixed blood which they first established in power; and our languages are dialects of their speech. But what we know we have learnt from the ancient Greeks: the method of our science is theirs, the principles of our art are theirs; and men became conscious of that debt at the Renaissance.

From that time not only did the past become an element in the conscious life of civilization, by the discovery of history, but the different sections of the human race began to be in continuous contact. Europe discovered the other parts of the world; China and India began to contribute ideas and experience to the composite we now call civilization. The history of civilization is not entirely a history of Europe. The labour and thought which have gone to the make of the future were not all contributed by our ancestors. But it is still too soon for us to estimate justly the contributions of peoples outside the European tradition; we may, therefore, continue for the present to assume that civilization, as we know it, is European.

Almost a thousand years have passed since the mediæval civilization reached its perfection; and the succession of the generations continues. We are part of the same pageant. We know much more than our forefathers—in so far as knowledge consists of information about described details of things and of our own lives. It is difficult in another sense of the word "know" to say that our biologists know more about a horse than the workers did who sculptured the frieze of the Parthenon or to say that our psychologists know more of human emotion than the butchers and bakers who played in the mystery plays. Descriptive knowledge, however, is greatly increased. A new form of power has come into our hands—not the power to sing or to build or to paint, but the power to move and to make; and this new power has led to an expansion of civilization.

The gain is great; but what proportion of living men share in it? Even the poorest, of course, are protected from some diseases by sanitation; the crumbs of food and rags of clothing, which are the surplus of civilized life, do fall to many more than had enough in the Middle Ages. But it is a fact, ascertained by statistical inquiry, that about twenty of every hundred persons in the industrial countries live in a state of poverty, which allows no provision against illness, no asylum for old age, no outlet for vitality, high intelligence or fine emotion. These twenty in every hundred are starved to death in the near presence of others who have a surfeit; and the majority have only a meagre share in civilization. The workers hardly know the value of the inheritance drawn from the labour of their forefathers which they may claim to share. The few rich are hardly aware that it is the labour of former generations which has made possible what they enjoy.

We live now in an era dominated by the machinery of manufacture and transport, in which the chief preoccupation of most men seems to be, not what they are doing, but what power to command services or enjoyments they can secure. Some are thus preoccupied because they can obtain a large supply of such power; but most men are obsessed with material cares because all their effort hardly yields enough power for them to live endurably. They live in continual dependence upon the will of others, and have no security for the future.

It is characteristic of our era that the greater part of the power to command services is in the hands of individuals who cannot be made to feel any public responsibility for the use to which it is put. This is called capitalism; and many evils are said to be caused by it. That we need not either affirm or deny. Undoubtedly some evils are due to this primitive method of organizing economic power; but the chief characteristics of our civilization are much older than this system, and the whole era of industrialism covers only about a hundred out of the three thousand years of European and the eight thousand years of recorded human history. Poverty and war, oppression, cruelty, and selfishness existed long before either industrialism or capitalism. On the other hand, the secular movement of common life, the life of workers with their hands and of thinkers, artists and dreamers, has gradually expanded, although sometimes checked and sometimes set back towards barbarism. Naturally the evils of our own day loom larger than evils already overcome, and therefore present discontent may make us blind to the great gains which have already been made.

But we must reckon our gains. We now control many diseases and have abolished some; we have secured the greater part of men from the danger of famine: we have diminished tyranny, oppression and cruelty in places where they once flourished. All this past is our inheritance. We cannot afford to imperil any of it, even though crying evils incite us to unthinking destruction. But, on the other hand, we cannot excuse the evil because of the good with which historically it was accompanied. The slavery of Greece was not less evil because of the design on an Attic coin from the mines of Laurium. The ignorance of mediævalism was not less evil because of the beauty of its architecture. If we claim our inheritance, therefore, we do not intend to sacrifice our lives for it, because the good in it will survive of its own force if we destroy the evil.

So much has been done: but even that cannot be understood unless we look at it in the doing and, as it were, before it was attempted. The canvas already covered seems obvious enough; but to understand what painting is, one should be able to see the bare canvas before the brush touched it. And if we see what has been done as the expression of dead men's hopes, we shall understand the more easily what may be done in the future. All that change from savage chaos to the temple and the cathedral is as nothing if compared to the changes that will occur in the future. How do we know? We know as those men knew who saw the temple in their mind's eye before it was built, or who felt the road as they cut the forest to make it.

Because those who build naturally look at what they are building, and not at the ground which supports them, the workers look more often to the future than to the past. Those who receive most benefit from the past are naturally its admirers, and are more tolerant of the evils it has left interspersed with the good it has done. The wealthier classes of to-day are more keenly aware of history than are the workers; but this awareness is vitiated by the tendency to regard history as what has happened. It is essential, however, to the mere understanding of the facts that we should view the past as, what it once was, a future. That is how the worker's view of history corrects the historian's. And when that is understood, then a new meaning is given to civilization. We see then that what we have inherited is the result of generations of labour; and we reckon our gain, not as a possession, but as an opportunity. Freedom from disease, famine or tyranny—that is the beginning of civilization. That is to say, a civilized man is one who lives vigorously with all his bodily and mental abilities; he is a man capable of fine emotion and keen intelligence in his work and in his leisure; and such a man could exist only in a company of such men. In our inheritance we have only the beginnings of that civilization. Our task, however, is not idly to admire our inheritance, but to make it the basis of our own achievement and thus to prove ourselves worthy heirs.

But what must we do to be worthy of it?

There are two methods by which we may make our conceptions clearer and our actions more effectual. One is to study and to feel the evils with which we have to contend, for that incites many to action. Those who do not themselves suffer greatly may need first to feel sympathy; for others, who are in fact limited or degraded by the conditions of their lives, it may be necessary to rise to a finer consciousness before they understand the injustice from which they suffer; for slaves do not always feel hurt by their slavery. Thus an awakening sense of evil may be the means to betterment. It is at any rate the natural and easy means for rhetorical politicians. The evils of the modern slum, of the dirt and ignorance, the superstitions of popular religion, and the meanness of the rich—these would be material for a conflagration. We could make a good bonfire of them and anything might set it alight.

There is, however, another way of strengthening our hands for the task which we vaguely feel they have it in them to do. That is to reach out towards the forms of what we desire. It is to fashion the shape of our hopes out of the best in our inheritance. What we achieve will not be like what we now imagine, but perhaps it will be better: and in any case the imagination will inspire the achievement.

First, we must displace economic terms from the precedence they have recently been given. Those who give their energies to the nationalizing of railways or the counting of calamities have their place—like the dukes and duchesses, who also are God's creatures. But their place is not the highest. The only purpose of nationalizing railways or obtaining control for the community over the means of production is that all men may sing and dance, and have eyes and ears for living. The energy spent upon the means should not obscure the end. The workers do not desire what only statisticians can understand. Their aim is indeed, in part, wealth; but if that sounds materialistic or crude, let the word be translated into the terms of a man's enjoyment and we shall see what has to be done. This is no mean desire nor mere jealousy. It is not that some who have little want to take from others the pearls and furs that they possess: it is that all men naturally and rightly desire whatever they can enjoy of beauty and fuller life. We must think of the civilization of the future, then, not mainly in economic terms, but by imagining men and women and children who are not deaf to music or blind to painting, who can talk skilfully and walk gracefully, who can dance and sing. But above all they must be able and eager to think freely and fearlessly; for it is reason, and not emotion, which has inspired men to build civilization. Reason has exalted our power over the world and chastened our arts. Reason is the basis and reason is the crown of the labour which makes men civilized. Reason will find the way to extend her gifts.

Who dares to say that what is fine can only be had by a few? Anyone who thinks he knows what is possible should consider what primitive man would have said of the possibility of flying, The achievements which are now in our minds are not so completely unlike what now exists as the facts of to-day are unlike the facts of a century ago, The will, therefore, is set towards a fuller enjoyment of a greater wealth, but more definitely towards the enjoyment than towards the wealth, for possibly a greater enjoyment of life may be available for all without additional pearls and furs. The demand of the workers is for civilization.

The next step is a more complete freedom for all workers to fulfil their function more adequately than is now possible. That will expand civilization. The amount of goods and services available will vastly increase and their quality immensely improve. A Greek temple or a mediæval cathedral may yet prove to be mere children's efforts by comparison to the noble buildings of a real community of free men and women. Halls for dance and song and drama open to all in the common service, far roads, wide spaces for wandering and, in the daily "business" of life, a dignity of surroundings and an ease of prevision —these will allow labour to be, what it naturally is, an outlet for enjoyed vitality.

This greatly increased amount of wealth need not be accompanied by deterioration in quality, if taste keeps pace with ability to produce. But that is a problem of education. In the industrial era education was almost a century behind manufacture, and worse than the industrial slum or the industrial magnate's house will befall us if we acquire new powers over nature before we are capable of using them. But the sense of new and loftier needs is already widespread. The education—limited as it was—of the past century is now having its effects. These effects are dangerous to the established order of morality, religion and industry. But in the danger is the opportunity. A new spirit is abroad. The Titan, Labour, who built the beginnings of civilization in his sleep, is half awakened. He stirs in his sleep like the Sons of Earth, and he may yet learn his own strength not to destroy, but to build more nobly.

II

FREEDOM

Manual labour, like thinking and emotion, is an expression of vitality. When any of these impulses or energies reaches its full natural growth, then it is free; and a man is free in whom all capacities for activity and enjoyment flow out to the extent of their strength. There is also a natural direction in the growth of a man's vitality as there is of a plant's. Labour and thought and emotion are like the springing of leaves, the blooming of flowers or the ripening of fruit; and as a flower is free which grows and swings in the wind to the extent and in the direction of its inner impulse, so labour and thought and emotion are free if they can be all that they have it in them to be. Hindrance and limitation of space and air and light deprive the flower of colour, and twist the tree into ungainly forms; and so poverty and tyranny and confusion may dwarf and cripple men.

The effort which has made civilization in its present form was as natural as the flow of the sap, and it has been so far free that it has had play within the area it has already covered. It might, therefore, be agreed that civilization depends more upon freedom than upon labour, for certainly what is best in our inheritance is due to that part of labour or thought which has been free. For that reason the earliest philosophers thought that leisure, and not labour, made civilization ; but Plato and Aristotle meant by leisure, not idleness, but energy self-directed and freely playing as contrasted with the energy exercised at command by a slave. In that sense leisure is essential ; but that is not the meaning of the leisure upon which those pride themselves who depend upon the labour of others for their daily bread. The ability to exercise imagination, to move out of the shadow of the past and to escape from the magic circle of the necessities of the present—all this is labour, and it can only be credited to leisure because this labour must be free. Labour is not a curse ; it is life. The Stoics and the writers of the New Testament began to see this, for there are truths in their writings which were unknown to men of much greater ability. But the confusing succession of new social discoveries in pre-modern Europe, and the discoveries of the facts of nature in our own time obscured the fundamental dependence of all civilization upon labour. We now realize a fact which was hardly noticed before, although it was fundamental in the very earliest civilization.

The freedom which is necessary for the exercise of labour or thought has been as little understood as labour itself. It has been assumed that freedom means the absence of limitation, which is correct but misleading ; for it explains by a negative, and has therefore led to the absurdities of individualism. In that theory the free man was the man without a setting, for it was forgotten that the value of freedom lies in the original impulse, and not in the absence of an obstacle. The positive conception of freedom displaces the idea of limitation by that of natural growth. The flower grows, not to a limit, but to its natural height. Secondly, the older idea of freedom assumed that each centre of life was an isolated, atomic unit, that the free man was the man by himself; and we now know that the vitality of every flower and every man is the life of all that has gone to make the new being. The flower is free by right of the seed and the soil; man is free by right of the society of which he is a part. But the change in the idea of freedom has come about not by abstract theorizing; it has been forced upon us by practical experience.

In the sphere of law and public administration the principles of freedom were discovered before they were applied to the workers. Freedom as well as equality and brotherhood were found to be valuable among themselves by the members of small privileged groups in ancient Greece and Rome; and after the practice of authority in the Middle Ages and the Renaissance, the French Revolution attempted to apply them to all men. But the basis of that Revolution was too abstract and its principles were never seriously applied to economic issues or to the position of women. Male workers, however, have in most countries entered into the privileges of the small "democratic" groups of the old world. The workers can influence law and public administration without any special effort in most Western countries. So far as this goes, the workers are free, although they have not yet used their freedom to control the political situation.

This partial freedom of the workers has been accompanied in some countries by the freedom of women. The ancient Greeks and other less intelligent races classed women with slaves; and some even in modern times have imagined that a woman is a defective man. Such laughable childishness cannot be disproved here: we note only that it survives in prejudices among manual workers who do not understand the worker's point of view. It is to be seen in the treatment of wives and in the hostility in some industries to women workers. But it is quite irreconcilable with the principle upon which the free organization of labour rests; for the freedom of women is necessary to the full life of the community, as Plato saw. Women, however, in the name of equality sometimes claim rights which in practice involve giving them a privileged position. Hostility to women workers in some industries is based upon the perception that the acceptance of a lower salary by women may involve their acquiring a privileged position and excluding or degrading other workers. It is not, therefore, only as a right of women that their freedom is claimed, but also as essential and in so far as it is essential for all who are not women in the exercise of their own freedom. The freedom of women of course implies not simply the right to a vote or a candidature, but entry to all occupations which women desire to enter as well as unfettered choice of companionship and in the exercise of their functions as women. Thus throughout civilized society all sane adults are in co-operation in the fullest possible use of their energies for the maintenance and development of civilized life. The defects or limitations of this freedom are largely due to ignorance of methods of social organization or inability to use old methods.

But the conception of freedom has been enlarged by a new experience. The manual workers in industry have a conception of freedom which absolutely displaces the theoretical ideas of individualism. The economist who learns his lessons from the banker thinks that the worker's freedom is restricted if he works according to a rule for the benefit of the slower or weaker worker. An absurd idea seems to prevail among those who do no manual work that each manual worker ought to expend all his energy without regard to the pace at which his fellows can work; but apart from the danger of cuts in the piece-work rates, which the workers have reason to fear, economically and socially the confusion and hindrances in industry would be much greater than they are if each worker had no regard for the others. Indeed, the workers have discovered in practice that the freedom of each is greater if his work "plays into the hands" of the other. Even the idlers in British society know that fact in games. The trade union in industry is based upon the fundamental principle that freedom is social and the government of trade unions has been the training-ground for labour politics.

The trade union was a social discovery of the manual workers in the new industrial era; and the experience so consolidated is now the source of increased vitality in the whole community. The daily lives of men in the mines or the shops, or of women in the mills, must be the basic experience, the analysis of which will provide the principles of social transformation. It is not, then, by understanding capitalism, but by understanding labour, that the limitations and defects of existing civilization will be destroyed. The manual workers have something of their own to contribute to the intelligence and the emotion which seeks release in a new and better world; and their first contribution is the conception of social freedom.

The defect of individualism is not merely that it conceives men as separate units, but that it conceives society as a juxtaposition and not as an interaction. In actual life the energy of one man flows into the energy of another, and the pull of two upon the same rope is more than the pull of each added to the pull of the other. Thus the life of any community is the flow of the energy of its members through the experience of all.

This physical energy, this activity, this thought, this emotion, is labour. The reasons for which it is done do not affect the fact that it is labour ; for even leisure is praised by the old philosophers only because it is an opportunity for a special kind of energy. We, however, are now able to see the common features of all human energy that is not wasted, whether or not advantages accrue from it to the actual person who expends the energy.

The conclusion must be obvious. The workers *are* the community. No valid contrast can be drawn between community and workers, for those who do no work have no part at all in the life of the community. Of course, we need not kill them nor even put them into asylums ; for we may be so benevolent as to keep them by our labour ornamentally idle. Thus " the perfect lady " may be preserved, as we keep a bird of paradise in the Zoo ; but she has no right to affect public policy. And if the workers alone are the community, it follows that the workers cannot ever be in the position of dictators. The dictator and his subject cannot be identical. The conception of a dictatorship is a survival of the obsolete theory of class, which is now replaced by the idea of a workers' community.

Of that community the life-blood is freedom.

Freedom means at least the ability to exercise whatever energy may be in a man; but obviously not all energies can be exercised to the same extent, because the excess of one interferes with the exercise of another. Thus the ability to drink may be indulged so extremely as to interfere with the ability to think. That man is free who can get as much out of himself as possible on the whole and in the long run; but this principle is inadequate if a man be assumed to be a separate unit, as Mill should have seen. If each man is assumed to be essentially separate from every other, then the presence or activity of other men appears to be a limitation or restriction of freedom. But man is not an atom, and the free man, therefore, cannot be essentially the man apart from other men. Freedom must imply some reference to social life. Our principle must be based, not upon the abilities of an abstract individual, but upon the energies of man in society, who is indeed the only actual man. The ability in a man is not only his own seeing and hearing, but his understanding of other men and being understood, his helping them and being helped. Thus when I make shoes for you, I extend your freedom; and when you tell me what you know, you extend my freedom. Freedom is essentially social: for the antisocial ability to do as I like irrespective of its effect on you is not freedom at all, not even my freedom. Thus the law which prevents my exploiting you by overwork or underpayment is not a restriction or limitation of freedom, as the ceasing to drink in order to think is not constraint. The law against exploitation or injury of others says in effect that no man is able to get all that is possible out of himself by exploitation. The law against theft or murder preserves the possible victim for the sake even of the possible thief or murderer. Thus the law promotes the freedom even of those who have the opportunity of exploiting or murdering others.

This conception of freedom is natural to those who work for their living, because they know, not in theory, but, as the phrase goes, in their very bones, that all work is co-operation. The knowledge of that fact is much more general now than it was in earlier and simpler ages. Large-scale manufacture has almost abolished the worker who finished a whole product with his own tools at his own cost; and some lament the fact that most modern workers make only part of a product with another man's tools and as part of a process the whole of which the worker never sees. But whatever has been lost in the new system, the fact that labour is a co-operation has become more obvious: and that is a gain. We can see now that men are free only when they work together.

The implications of this conception of freedom should be clear. Such freedom cannot exist without the open expression and criticism of every kind of opinion, the active use of every road to possible truth; for it is assumed that truth is not altogether known and may in any section of experience not be known at all. It goes without saying that every civilized man is responsible for his expression or criticism of opinion. Freedom also involves that full information is available and intelligible, but of course not without the effort which a civilized man is bound to make to obtain it. Again, freedom involves the ability of every man to combine or associate with any other for the promotion of any policy. Without these the fundamental characteristics of a workers' society are not and cannot be realized.

It follows that tyranny and war are objectionable. Tyranny within a society involves suppression of criticism, the maintenance of spies, and the possible constraint of individuals or of minorities. This is bad, even if it is done as a means to a good end such as efficient production, for tyranny cannot be a means to freedom; and it is worse when tyranny is exercised in the name of "the people" than when it is in the name of God, for it may deceive the people into supporting its methods if it claims to speak in their name.

Similarly, war and the preparation for war involve suppression of divergent views in a community, the practice of deceit directed against the enemy but also affecting one's own people and the loss of moral responsibility for their acts by soldiers and perhaps by a whole population. War and freedom cannot be combined; and now at last we see that the freedom of one nation cannot be developed without increasing the freedom of all others. The rule of social freedom which governs the relation between members of the same community also governs the relation between the members of one community and all members of other communities; for no one of them can be free except by the use of the free energies of all the others. This, of course, does not mean that the workers will not join in a war or in the preparation for war so long as the alternative is an absence of any political organization governing the relationship between nations; but it does mean that freedom can be realized only when such international organization exists. This is implied in the present situation; but the workers are not generally conscious of the fact. They feel an annoyance at being called upon occasionally to leave their ordinary occupations because foreigners are said to be meditating some injury to them; for the normal workers want to "get on with the job." But the political system of modern times does not permit any man to live without responsibility for his own fate.

In the development of civilization various systems for developing political freedom have been used. In ancient Greece and Rome direct rule of the free was often practised. In the Middle Ages this was mixed with the new system of representation. Now in many Western countries a system is in vogue which may be called representative Parliamentary Democracy. This system has proved useful in many ways, and it has been gradually modified for the better; but it has certain grave defects. The "franchise" or the right to representation in legislative bodies is old-fashioned, for it is still generally based upon property, and not upon labour; and, from what has been said above, it will be seen that the only person with a right to vote is the person who contributes some energy of his own to the common life. But this does not imply that any sane adults should be without a vote, nor even that the vote should be non-territorial. It implies only that the whole community must be regarded as a community of those contributing their own thought or energy to the common life. Again, the candidature is old-fashioned, for it is practically impossible for men who are not wealthy unless they exist on terms or under necessities which may be oppressive. Again, there is no open representation of groups other than the territorial, for example social and economic "functions." Again, in most countries the centralization of government is extreme; and in some countries there are obsolete Chambers or authorities.

All this criticism is not made in behalf of a political theory, but for the sake of the manual and other workers who are hampered by the defects of the instrument they have inherited. But that does not involve throwing away the instrument, unless it cannot be sharpened. It is worth while to try to put a new edge on the old blade. It does not, of course, follow that Parliamentary Democracy is the only possible method of maintaining or promoting freedom. Local traditions or circumstances define what method is best; and although among us Westerners the Parliamentary method may be good, we cannot prescribe it for all other peoples at all times, nor can we reasonably maintain that it will always remain the best for us. It is undeniable that under this system slavery has been abolished and the workers have attained power to associate in trade unions and other societies. So far, therefore, we work with it and hope for the best.

The basis of the system needs a fuller examination than could be attempted here. The mythology of voting will probably be dispelled by advances in social psychology; but even now it is clear that counting votes is not counting persons, but sounding the strength of opinions. The ten thousand who vote for one man do not express ten thousand opinions, but one opinion: and it is quite irrelevant whose opinion it is. It usually originates in one man or a small group. We test its persuasiveness crudely by counting votes; but nobody imagines that that is a test of its truth.

The governing factor, however, in political life is not the system, but the social atmosphere; and that is still in Western countries full of obsolete admirations for wealth and rank or title. In such an atmosphere freedom is hardly able to grow. The fundamental problem, therefore, is how to change the atmosphere by establishing in power, not the workers as a class, but the worker's point of view.

III

THE WORKER'S POINT OF VIEW

If the worker's point of view were dominant in any society, there would be a transformation of the idea of work and therefore a reorganization in the practice of work. That point of view, however, is reached, not by abstract theory, but through the experience of the majority of workers who are, in all ages, manual workers; and the worker's point of view must therefore be primarily the position of those who work with their hands. But since all forms of human energy are in one sense labour, there will be no opposition between the handworker and the thinker.

The consciousness that a new social order is possible undoubtedly begins as a consciousness of class. The workers, although in fact they are the community, feel themselves to be set over against other persons or groups; and this opposition to others—the natural effect of bitter experience—would prevent their contributing anything great to civilization if it were not accompanied, as it is, by a pride in skill and a keen sense of human fellowship. The class-consciousness of the workers has the same elements of primitiveness and of moral excellence which were in the class consciousness of those who once said: *Noblesse oblige.* The workers, like the aristocracy of an earlier age, begin to feel not only that they have rights because labour made civilization, but also that they have duties because civilization depends for its continuance upon them. The worker's point of view implies that a railwayman, an engineer, a textile worker or a dustman is bound by the honour of his calling. He cannot bring himself to do certain acts, and certain difficult tasks he feels bound to endure. There is pride in it; but that sort of pride is a virtue. Pride in the work one does, and claims to rights on the ground of work performed or still to be undertaken, have always existed. What is new is the consciousness of this spreading through the whole class of manual workers. We must look, then, to the characteristics of manual work itself to discover the meaning of the worker's point of view.

First, there is the sense of the free play of energy in manual labour. This is a well-known psychological fact. The muscular sense is distinct from the sense of touch or sight or smell. It is a feeling of expansiveness, of exaltation of the personality which cannot possibly be derived from reading books or calculating. It is a sense of the body alive. In a modern industrial community those who dominate intellectually are so far separated from the physical contact with the earth and from the muscular experience of the labour upon which civilization depends that they tend to forget or to underrate the essential characteristics of manual labour.

One can hear in any coalfield the chance words of scorn of the "slacker," the man who cannot "go all out" on a face of coal. Not that the miner despises physical weakness. He is well aware that one man may be less vigorous than another. That is not the point. The slacker is the man who does not bring his muscles into play—whatever muscles he has. He may "slack" in order to get something for nothing—and some men in all classes do—or he may "slack" because of some mysterious theory. The point is that he deliberately does less than proves him a man, and is therefore despised by his fellows. Similarly, the turner or fitter in an engineering shop, or the engine-cleaner, or the locomotive driver, does not in fact go slow or scamp his work as the searcher after increased profits may believe—and the proof of it is that civilization still exists. If the workers were as unwilling as some would have us believe, there would be little enough good steel or machinery, and no trains running to their destinations. But it is often inconvenient to recognize obvious facts—such a fact, for example, as that civilization is borne up by the manual workers. These workers themselves know it. They feel it in the stretch of their muscles and the life of their eyes; and others can know it if they watch the engine-driver or the man at the lathe.

Secondly, the worker's point of view implies the recognition of the social necessity of the work he does. He feels himself a man in his work not merely in his own body, but in the effects of his work upon other men. This is no theoretical economics or hypothesis that labour is the sole source of wealth; it is the simple observation of the dependence of men in society upon the work done for the upkeep of society. Perhaps there are some leisured and cultured persons in our "select" residential districts, who inhabit what is called either bijou or baronial, who really believe that the engine-driver or the dustman does his work without thinking about it. Descartes, that very select philosopher, thought birds were automata; and those who get their ideas and emotions from a lending-library seem to imagine that manual workers are automata. But speak to dustmen or railway-guards or coal-miners, and you will find the sense of the social value of work done very widely appreciated among them. It is almost a physical sense of the unity of the acts which go to make up civilization.

Thirdly, the workers feel companionship with those who work beside them. This is the source of the trade-union spirit. Compare a trade-union shop with one from which the unicn is excluded; in the second you will feel the suspicion of each man against his fellows, the continual watchfulness of the atomic individual lest advantage should be taken of him, the strain of isolation. In a union shop, of course, individual hostilities may survive, but in general the workers feel that there is some organization, some method for guarding their interests, and they are, therefore, calmer and more friendly. The results on industry are still insufficiently appreciated, because unions are still conceived both by their members and by outsiders as chiefly associations for opposition or battalions of an army. Here, however, we are concerned with the fellow-feeling which the almost physical sense of contiguity in the workshops has produced. This fellow-feeling is characteristic of manual workers and is not so common among artists or organizers or thinkers; but this very feeling is one of the most valuable elements in social life which is underestimated by those who make their political attitude out of theories. That is why a working-class party introduced a new factor in politics.

It has often been remarked that the British Labour Party arose out of trade unionism, and it still depends upon the trade unions, not only for its funds, but for its vitality. Some lament this, for they think of politics in the old terms of political science and not in the new terms of political psychology. The chief value of the British experience is that a workers' party has come into existence by the pressure of natural impulse among the rank and file of the workers, and not by the creation of theorists. The association of workers conscious of one another as workers is the ground of the characteristic worker's point of view which has been carried from the industrial into the political field by the British Labour Party.

Finally, even workers who do not understand the worker's point of view know very well that manual labour is generally in its essence "mental." No worker thinks of himself as a tool. The engine-cleaner or the weaver at the loom, although his work be repetition, knows that he is using his mind. The workers by hand are also workers by brain, in one sense at least. Indeed, many of those who read other people's books are more "mechanical" in their behaviour than the unlettered shepherd or docker. The manual workers, therefore, may accept fellowship with those whom we do not class as manual workers, such as the painter, the musician and the surgeon, and even with the journalist "driving" his mechanical quill; but that does not involve a submission of the manual workers to superior persons. It should be the admission on each side of the honourable necessity of the work of the other. The worker's point of view involves the admission of all work as in some sense human, and therefore not merely instrumental or manual without being mental; but it also involves the recognition of a common spirit and impulse between the manual worker and the artist, the writer or the administrator.

By this time some readers will be annoyed. They will feel defrauded of the luxury of woe which some indulge by the recitation of other people's grievances. They will say that the workers are wronged—that they need social reform, old-age pensions, unemployment insurance and workmen's compensation, and that the desire for these is the fundamental issue for "progressive" parties. No one denies that evils exist from which the manual workers suffer more than any other class. No one denies that these evils must be diminished and eventually destroyed by "progressive" legislation or, better still, by improved industrial organization. But some reformers misunderstand the worker's point of view so completely that they expect all those workers who suffer to be grateful for benevolent gifts. In the name of progress benevolence is increased, and the reformers sometimes find their gifts and their professions of sympathy flung back into their faces. They then weep over the dividing of "the forces of progress." They say that social reformers desire the same improvements in existing society as the representatives of the working class, and that the two groups should work together. They are entirely wrong. They misunderstand altogether the mind of the workers, for they misinterpret the worker's desire for reforms.

Two men may agree to cross a river by the same bridge, and one of them may aim at keeping the bridge open for a return, while the other aims at finding a new home on the farther side. To the former the bridge, to the latter the farther bank, is more important. Their disagreement is more fundamental than their agreement in regard to immediate policy.

From the worker's point of view the evils of the present are merely symptoms; and to confine policy to a mere treatment of symptoms is a mistake in the curative art. We must diagnose and deal with the disease underlying the symptoms. We must, of course, treat symptoms, lest the patient dies while we are preparing the cure; but our medicine and surgery must be somewhat more radical than social reform. We must, therefore, re-interpret the meaning of those evils to which we have referred—impoverished old age, semi-starvation during unemployment, and ruin following accidents. All these grow out of the one great evil of degrading poverty, which stunts or twists the body, narrows the mind, and deadens nobility of emotion. There is no question here of the fact that some have less money than others: the real problem arises only from the fact that a great number have not the bare means for a humane life. It is further remarkable—although the majority do not think it strange—that it is the manual workers who suffer from this degradation. If old ladies with nothing to do suffered semi-starvation, if artists who could not sell their works had no resources—that might be distressing, but it would not be socially absurd. But that workers on whom civilization depends for its food and machinery should be refused the bare means of rendering their services efficiently—that is utterly ludicrous. And the flagrant defects of the industrial system are made still more obvious by the riches which are allowed to accrue to persons who render no service at all. Even liberal-minded reformers seem to imagine that we cannot help ourselves; that some natural law necessitates the waste and incompetence of contemporary social life; and the mythology of an obsolete pseudo-science makes those who profess to be helpless into supporters of a transitory, accidental system of bad habits.

From the worker's point of view society is essentially a co-operative enterprise in which the status and rights of each depend upon the function each performs. And by his existence in society a man has not merely the duty, but the right to perform some function. That is the meaning of the old claim "the right to work." A man's political rights should depend upon his place in the whole co-operative enterprise of social life. The purely economic organization is not now in question; for quite apart from the exchange of commodities and services, every function a man performs is part of the life of society—for example, the functions of parent or husband or teacher or poet or administrator or judge, quite as much as the function of railwaymen or weaver, make up society.

The grievances, therefore, of the manual workers, from the worker's point of view, involve a claim to rights, not a request for charity. The worker protests, not that the employers or the public are unkind, but that the social system is unjust. The grievances are widespread, and they strike deep into the lives of the workers; and no one in any social class can appreciate the worker's point of view without a keen feeling of the injustice involved in the conditions under which the majority live and work. But sympathy for suffering is not enough. Nor is hate of oppression enough. The fundamental impulse which moves the workers is a deep and determined resolve to have done with the causes of suffering and oppression. That is what is meant by the "class war." We are not playing at politics. The retention of the power to oppress by small groups of rich persons, and the inertia which ignores the suffering of others, are themselves forms of war. The working classes do not "declare war." They are suffering from the effects of a state of war maintained for the advantage of others: and it would indeed be foolish for them to advocate war as a policy because in fact they suffer from its effects.

It follows from the character of the impulse towards justice that the workers are more deeply concerned with their work than with their leisure. Their political status as well as their economic power arises from the services they perform, not from their opinions or enjoyments in their "spare" time. But few appreciate what a fundamental issue is here involved. It is nothing less than a moral transformation of the attitude towards work. The worker's point of view can never triumph so long as work is regarded as a curse or a burden which no one could be induced to undertake without an "incentive." The theory of the worker as an ass to be goaded forward by the prick of starvation or enticed forward by the carrot of higher wages is a fantastic creation of economists who picked up their psychology from bankers. It does not represent the fundamental characteristics of work.

Work is in essence an enterprise, an adventure, an outlet for energy, a form of vitality; secondly, it is a binding force of society, a service, a co-operation, a fellowship. No one denies that in actual practice to-day some work is degrading and much work is depressing; but that is because of the system under which men now drive locomotives or add columns of figures. Regularity need not be monotony, obedience to directions need not be a renunciation of all will or interest in what is done. Therefore work is what the worker desires, but of course on condition that it is free and not slavish. With that fire of work the new world may be built out of the chaos of existing conflicts. It is not, however, to be assumed that this view of work is accepted or understood by the majority of workers in any society. Some have never perceived the implied distinction between two views of labour. These do not think at all in general terms. They can see the distinction between a lawyer in a top hat and a navvy in a cloth cap ; but they cannot see the distinction between one navvy and another. The greater number of any social class are unconscious of the assumptions which they inherit or accept uncritically from others. But there are some manual workers who are conscious, at least vaguely, of themselves as distinguishable from members of other classes. These make a first step, but do not go far. They feel their distinctiveness and, like the fox without a tail, they jump to the conclusion that what is different from them must be worse than they. They are hostile to members of other social classes with the simple hostility to what is strange ; but they have not yet grasped the true value of their own position.

A still smaller group really have the worker's point of view. They bear themselves proudly, not because of their difference from others, but because of the need that others have for them. These are fully conscious of the meaning of labour. They make claims to rights which are very different from requests for benevolence and therefore sound like battle-cries ; but they do not hate or despise men whose speech or dress differs from theirs. The contrast between those who have the worker's point of view and those who have not cuts deep into the life of a community; it must not be confused with the trivial contrast between manual workers and the rest of the world. There are, of course, millions of workers who accept a point of view implying the subordination of themselves and their work to superior persons, and some of these may have strayed into organizations whose spirit is dominated by another ideal. The fundamental fact is not that a man is or is not a manual worker; what is fundamental is the attitude he takes to the work he does.

Take as an example a shipwright or an engine-driver. Such a man may be proud of the position his work gives him: he may feel himself to be in his work an element of the life of the community. He may claim rights which rest upon the need of the public for the performance of his task, for he can truly assert that without adequate security and well-being he cannot be an efficient servant of the community. But the ground of all his professed opinions or claims will be the sense of his own value as a contributor to the common good. He has the worker's point of view.

On the other hand, a shipwright or an engine-driver may despise his own position and have a low estimate of the work he has to do. He may endure working simply as a means to obtain a livelihood. In that case he will accept the traditional conception of caste in society, and in the process of "looking up" to his superiors he may turn his back upon himself. He has respect for others; but little self-respect, and no respect at all for the class to which he belongs. Such a man, although a manual worker, has *not* the worker's point of view. The fact that he works with his hands for a weekly wage does not interfere with his being a good conservative, an admirer of old times, his master's man. He is not wicked or ignorant because he does not take the worker's point of view. It may, indeed, be to his interest to "better" himself by spurning his fellows; but he is set upon the ancient ways, and has no part in the building of a new world.

The domination of the worker's view over the whole of a society can only take place when the greater part of the workers themselves, or at least the most vigorous group among them, understand and appreciate the meaning of freedom and labour. The crucial problem, therefore, is educational; but it is not a problem of educational systems or textbooks. It is a problem which can only be solved by the practical expansion of intelligence over the whole field of labour, so that there shall be no longer any distinction between workers and thinkers. In plain words, the workers must be able and willing to think, not by proxy or by the assistance of any intellectual caste, but by themselves.

IV

THE INTELLECTUALS

THE test of intelligence is the capacity to learn, not the skill to teach. Therefore the function of the intelligent in any society does not give them any right to adopt a superior air. They should be good listeners, or at any rate more ready to listen than to speak; and if they speak, they should regard it as the highest praise that they should be believed to be saying what everyone else means. Indeed, in any nation or in any group within a nation the domination of a caste of intellectuals is the worst of all tyrannies because it is the most efficient, if such a tyranny can secure itself against criticism by making its critics feel their own incompetence.

As a preliminary, then, it must be understood that there is no excuse for the existence of a class or caste of persons distinguished from others as intellectuals, having a special education or special opportunities of culture, just as there is no excuse for a class of the excessively rich or unendurably poor. Of course there will always be in any community some who are wiser than others; there will always be some who have a better education because they are better able to acquire what education gives. But they need not, and, in a healthy community, they could not, constitute a special class or caste. They will be members of the different groups performing functions within the community, and they will differ from other members of their groups only as a philosophic or musical railwayman may differ from a railwayman who has no appreciation of philosophy or music. The intellectuals, in this sense of the word, have a task to perform both within their own groups and in the community as a whole, but they cannot perform it by cutting themselves off from the group to which they belong or adopting a superior air.

The part to be played by those who have a ready wit, a good memory or ability to reason quickly, is certainly not less honourable than the part of the coal-miner or of the woman at the loom. A proper pride in good thinking is as necessary to the thinker as pride in his art is essential to the potter. It may, indeed, be sometimes useful to insult those who say that they are " practical " because they find it difficult to see anything not immediately under their noses; for there is a prejudice against all thought which can show no tangible results. An old-fashioned Revolution once led to the absurd belief that " the Republic had no need of chemists "; and some modern revolutionaries seem to hate nothing more than criticism of themselves. There is also an inherited superstition that action tends to be " sickled o'er with the pale cast of thought "—which is, no doubt, based upon the fact that some who claim to be thinking are really dreaming. Further, there is a primitive economic theory which underrates the importance of what is not obviously physical activity; for a navvy picking up the road sometimes foolishly supposes that a man watching a bird by the wayside is doing nothing. But the navvy in that attitude is thinking—not fulfilling his function as a physical force. The navvy, therefore, cannot condemn thinking without condemning in the same breath the very process which he is using when he condemns. Sometimes the trade-union leader, too, needs to be reminded of this, even if he may not be able to understand the point of it. It is silly to offer a bad theory as the ground for condemning all theory. The Republic needs chemists ; the Revolution needs poets; the State needs saints ; the counting-house needs philosophers ; Labour needs artists. All these are expressions in different forms of the place of the intellectuals in a civilized society.

These assertions, however, may be obscure without commentary. Precisely what is the need to which we refer ? The need is similar to the need of one leg for the other, if walking is to be normal. You may hop into Revolution, and equally well into Reaction : but walking is the mode of progression towards civilized life—always granted that two legs may also be used to run with, if you are in training and do not lose your breath. The need for intelligence is as fundamental as the need for physical well-being or strength.

First, there is, as we have said above, no fundamental distinction between manual and mental work. All manual work is in some sense mental unless it becomes less than human, and then it should be abolished. Similarly, all mental work is in some sense bodily : any textbook of psychology will give the proof of that. But if thinking is bodily, it is in the very simplest sense "labour" ; that is to say, it has all the fundamental characteristics of what every man calls work. For some, no doubt, thinking requires a difficult and distasteful effort ; others cannot help themselves—they *must* think, as some men *must* move about and cannot keep still.

Thinking in all its forms is natural life and not a disease.

Secondly, thinking in all its forms—perception, memory, reasoning, imagination—is an integral part of a whole which is human activity. Thinking cannot safely be separated from doing other things besides thinking. Any treatise on education will give the proof of that. And as in the individual thought should always be accompanied by other action, so in a civilized community the contact between those who chiefly think and those who chiefly do other things should be intimate and continuous. This is to restore thought to its place in the life of a society, to prevent its becoming a dilettante tickling of minor nerve centres. But to give this position to thought is essential from the worker's point of view, for thought is thus a part of "labour" which goes to the make of civilized life. Thinking is more like manual labour than it is like inheriting or keeping wealth. There is no fundamental distinction of function or of life between the manual workers and the intellectuals unless we are to allow the name "intellectual" to the hangers-on in drawing-rooms and the superficial commentators on gossip.

Thirdly, it follows that thinking cannot be the function of an exclusive caste, still less a function which can be inherited. Any man at any time may think, and such thought must be gathered up and used just as much as the thought of the few who think more often or more continuously. But the ability to think differs in different men, irrespective of their position in the community; and ability to think is a native *trait*, just as much as skill with the hands. Such *traits* may be inherited—we know too little of heredity to say how or when; but obviously we cannot take it for granted that the son of a good scholar will be himself a good scholar. Therefore in each generation the opportunities should be equal for all to know whether each can think. This is the fundamental basis for the connection between a bold educational policy and the ideals implied in the worker's point of view. So necessary for a worker's world is the function of real thought in all its forms that we cannot afford to risk the loss of any genius which may appear in any section of society: and therefore all the new generation must be given full opportunity to give signs of ability or genius.

Suppose it, then, to be granted that the intellectuals have an important function to perform, and that means must be taken to correct the present obstacles to its performance, how are such intellectuals as at present exist to conduct themselves?

It has already been said that their chief function is *not* to look after other people's business. Unfortunately some intellectuals too readily appoint themselves to be guides of those who are less talkative. The self-appointed reformer often tells people what they ought to do without any knowledge of what they are actually doing—which is often better than the reformer's proposal. Thus persons who know nothing of the schools often tell the teachers to improve methods which have long since become obsolete; and persons who know nothing of trade unions tell the workers to stop doing what is no longer done. This causes the victims to be impolite to their advisers. On the other hand, the outside public, hearing the voice of the self-styled intellectuals, foolishly imagines that they are leading the groups for which they only too volubly speak. This is to mistake the big drum-stick for the conductor's baton. Even in revolutions the deeper changes are not to be discovered in the language of the leaders.

In any civilized community those with exceptional genius should have free play. The test of what a man should do cannot be merely that any other man could do it, and indeed the more civilized we become the greater the variety of activities becomes which cannot be duplicated, the greater the number of persons recognized to be unique. That is why any such crude test as examination is almost useless—" the nightingale got a fourth class at the fowl show." There should be more artists, if perhaps fewer who try to make a living out of art. But we cannot test for art except by giving a man the opportunity of attempting art. There is no preliminary test.

Now, administration and the direction of policy may require an exceptional genius which the majority of men are not able to test. The majority may not understand even their own interests in far-reaching policies, and may be quite incapable of choosing the right person for directing their affairs. Are we, therefore, condemned by the nature of things to a dictatorship by those who can assert their own competence? All dictatorship is objectionable. To dictate in the name of the proletariat is no better than to dictate in the name of the nation or of God. Neither God nor the nation nor the proletariat is given a fair chance under such a régime. Still, if there were no real alternative, we should accept dictatorship.

The vote of the majority is not a preferable alternative, for that indicates at most only a vague tendency of public taste, not the reasoned choice between opposed policies. Besides, any competent dictator can obtain the vote of the majority, and therefore it may not be a real but only a sham alternative to dictatorship. Plebiscites in history have been often the registers of the will of one man. Free elections are often only the unconscious submission of crowds to the dominating ideas of small groups. The argument, therefore, against tyranny does not necessarily support the prevailing practices of Western politics. There may be, however, some place and time at which dictatorship is less evil than any possible alternative; and there are certainly some uses in the vote of the majority as a general guide. The distinction, in any case, between a dictatorship and a majority vote is not clear enough to guide us in deciding upon the function which the intellectuals should perform.

The function of intellectuals may be defined as that of leading or of criticism. Leaders and critics are among the most necessary servants of Labour and of the community; but both functions need further definition. Leading has two aspects—interpretation and speculative provision. As interpreters, leaders may be representatives or delegates. They do not "represent" in the sense of being substitutes for what they represent; for they ought not to be mirrors or echoes. Representation as a social function is like the representation of a sound by a letter: it is an activity in one sphere having a correspondence with another activity in another sphere. The true representative is an artist having a sense of the group for which he stands, but that sense need not have been present to the consciousness of any member of the group. A false democracy may be dissatisfied with a representative for being unlike any member of the group, and so we have had absurd examples of mere members of the group being taken as representatives. A real representative in a real democracy is something different, not necessarily superior nor wiser than his individual constituents, but somehow having another type of ability. There is, further, no *a priori* method of discovering what group or what persons or what interests can or should be represented. That will depend upon the characteristics of the group. Any group *may* develop the capacity of being truly and effectually represented; and similarly an individual may show capacity for representing this or that. But it is childish to decry representation because attempts at obtaining it have been sometimes ludicrous, sometimes pernicious.

Another form of interpretation is done by a delegate: but he too is not a mirror, for it is impossible even in the case of delegation to foresee exactly the issue which the delegate may have to face. The ability to be a delegate requires a better memory but a less vivid imagination than that of a representative. The delegate says what he is told to say. His function is more limited and of shorter duration; but again, not every man can be a good delegate. Both in the case of the representative and in that of the delegate, what they "stand for" is not Mr. Smith and Mr. Jones, the individuals taken separately, but Mr. Smith in relation to Mr. Jones, who may in that relation be more irritable or more foolish or more wise than he otherwise appears to be. In any case all this depends upon the existence of something which used to be called the "will" of the group or "the people"; but that something is now seen to be more like impulse, "set" or tendency than like will. To render this in administration, in legislation or in the organization of industry is an art of which we have only the first elements; and youthful or cynical impatience often mistakes the crudity of our efforts in Western civilization for fundamental errors of policy or doctrine. Short cuts may indeed lead to other ends—such as efficient tyranny—but there is no other way than democracy towards organized liberty.

But leaders are not altogether interpreters: some perform the function of eyes to the rest of the body politic. These see issues which are not yet actual to the perception of the majority. They are like the persons who, Plato says, go up out of the cave and come back among men with their eyes still dazzled by the light of the sun. They are interpreters in the sense that they express the unconscious desires of the group to which they belong and its fears and premonitions. They are often more emotional than intellectual. They move people to follow them by the attraction of hope, not by persuasion based upon evidence. The imitators of this type of leader are the demagogues and the wild enthusiasts who never stop to think; and occasionally these imitators have deluded great numbers, but generally they attract only a small group of those who are constitutionally dyspeptic, unbalanced or light-headed. The normal man cheers them on, but he stays behind when they move forward, for he knows that not every forward move is a move in the right direction.

The intellectual functions so far described are well enough recognized among the workers; but there are other functions of the intelligent less generally understood. There is, for example, criticism. The value of criticism of one's self by another is the last thing learnt by an educated man; and simple-minded crowds easily mistake a critic for a traitor. But the worker's point of view cannot be developed at all unless there is criticism in all its forms directed to the habits, the beliefs and the hopes of the actual workers of to-day. Criticism has three forms: it may be adverse, it may be constructive, giving detailed plans by adjustment of differences, and it may be, finally, speculative in the sense that it turns away from present defects towards an ideal. In all these cases emotion, no doubt, plays a part; but the greater part is played by exact and resolute thinking. First, for adverse criticism—a devil's advocate of reaction is always useful. Reformers, and still more revolutionaries, tend to forget minor good which is sometimes living humbly in the midst of evil, like flowers on a dunghill. The adverse critic of what the workers demand will remind them that they are mortal—thus speaking as the slave who followed Cæsar in his triumph. But further, the actual workers are sometimes drunken, ignorant, ill-tempered, superstitious; and the whole body of workers needs to be reminded that men so limited cannot even conceive a worthy ideal.

Secondly, criticism is the function of those who carry out in the form of law or organization the desires of the community or of such groups within the community as have definite desires. The need for that is obvious.

Finally, the intellectuals must imagine intelligently. That is not merely seeing the sun outside the cave of common life and keeping the memory of it alive; it is the more difficult task of giving shape by skilful art to the road along which future generations may travel. This is the function of what Comte called "the spiritual power"; and these men and women are the teachers. All teachers should be part of the association in that spiritual power; but some who are by genius teachers make the very body and soul of those yet unborn. The experience and hopes of all willing workers in whatever sphere are sublimated in these men and women. They are the growth-point in social life. They are not leaders, for they work best when they are unknown and unnoticed; but a civilized society will have a sense of their presence, and will give due power to their influence.

V

THE STANDARD OF LIFE

The first task of the intelligence is the establishment of a civilized standard of life. In a world in which the worker's point of view is dominant, the enjoyments of all will be simple; for it is impossible to imagine a future in which there will be enough services and commodities available for all to be millionaires. There is no prospect of a community of Rockefellers or of Rothschilds. Of course, to-day the very rich are remarkable, not for the amount of the services they command, but for the difference between their economic power and that of the majority; but there are some reformers who seem to imply that the "career open to talents" should mean the possibility for each man to become a millionaire. Thus some forms of democracy are praised because they are opportunities for the enrichment of the individual; and apart from the simple selfishness of the attainment by one of what distinguishes him from the rest, there seems to be a vague feeling that if all had the opportunity of riches, all would fare well. In the United States this simple belief seems to be widespread; and wherever the pressure of poverty is continuous, riches are naturally accepted as the only tangible ideal.

Against this, and in spite of the acknowledged

excellence of economic wealth, we must boldly assert that a community without millionaires would be a happier and a finer community. It is no proof of the excellence of England that there are more rich men or greater opportunities of enrichment in England than in China, nor is it a proof of the value of riches that some have too much and others not enough to eat. The real problem of riches is not the need to have enough, for that all sensible men acknowledge. What is in question is the possession of a superfluity by a few who have no need to think of the cost of what they use. That is private riches, and that cannot be attained by all in any conceivable community; but so long as that is desired by a majority, the standards of the rich will dominate society; for the poor are enslaved, as Lucian said, not by their lack of wealth, but by their own admiration for the wealthy. That admiration must be destroyed.

To destroy the admiration for riches, however, may require not only the education of taste, but also an economic policy, which aims at preventing the accumulation of great wealth in private possession. If all the available wealth of any society were redistributed so that each would have an equal amount, of course no one might be noticeably richer. There may not be at present anywhere enough to increase to any important extent the wealth of each member of a large community; but that is irrelevant to our argument. If there is so little available, we ought to be all the more careful in our distribution of it. But far more important than the effect of a more equal distribution on the wealth of each is the effect upon the status and personality of each. A society without great differences among its members in the control of wealth would be a more civilized society.

It is for the sake of justice, not for the sake of the poor, that exceptional private wealth is condemned. But it must further be noted that a society in which all had even a little more would be far more energetic and productive in every sense than our society is to-day, for if a greater number had even a little more they would have more vitality. We are willing, therefore, to aim at private simplicity of life in a new society. But it must be understood that the absence of private accumulations of wealth in a civilized society does not imply the lack of wealth in large units for the use of society and under the control of public agents. A society of men living simply in private might be a society of great economic power held in common, as we shall explain later. The real issue is not the existence of wealth, but control of its use; for private ownership is only obstructive to civilization in so far as it prevents the use of wealth for public purposes.

We assert, then, that the standard of life in a worker's world must be simple. This implies a definite limit to the number of services and commodities a man or woman will possess or use. We do not imagine any legislation against luxuries, nor any sumptuary police regulations. We do not suppose that civilized men could ever endure the inquisition of officials into their private enjoyments, nor do we leave the smallest power to preachers against "vanities." The simplicity of the standard of life in a worker's world will be the result of a general taste, and of a social standard supported by the subtle influence of public opinion. It will be unseemly to be rich. Those who understand the worker's point of view will feel ashamed to demand extensive services or to use innumerable commodities.

They will be artists in the use of the simplest means to express the most civilized life. They will reject wealth because it hampers them, just as the athlete strips to run or to row. And public opinion, which embodies the worker's point of view, will look askance at ostentation. It will not be possible to accept services or use commodities without thinking of the labour which goes to the making of them; and men will refuse to use slaves even if they have the power to do so.

Obviously such a standard of life will be much more common throughout a community than any standard can be to-day; for as wealth is now distributed, there must be very diverse standards in existence side by side. Thus there is the standard of fashionable society with its fantastic waste. There is the business man's standard, involving possession of a car and a country house and a wife occasionally decorative. There is the standard of the lower middle class with its unused front parlour, its lace curtains and decaying plants; and there is the standard of the higher ranks of manual labour, with its small stuffy rooms and cracked pianos. None of these rather pitiful attempts at civilization should be despised. They are more pathetic than objectionable. Even the waste of the rich is a pathetic attempt by the uneducated to be thought civilized. They buy pictures they cannot see and hire music they cannot hear. But all industrial civilization is childish in its tastes, in spite of its careful segregation of the community into castes based upon income. The best taste is bad taste, where all are not free to indulge it.

The new standard of life will be operative throughout the whole community. There will be greater equality—not necessarily of spending power, but of actual enjoyment; for indeed Aristotle was right—we must equalize, not the possessions of men, but their tastes, and this education alone can do. The homogeneity of the extent, however, to which taste can be indulged in a whole community must not be supposed to necessitate identical tastes in every man; for although all may have some power to spend, and none may be allowed by public opinion to exceed a certain limit in spending, each man will have his own use for his economic power. A community of men more equal in wealth than ours will not be a monotonous society. Men will not dress alike or live alike even if they have the same extent of the power to dress and live. This is a fundamental point in regard to equality which the opponents of democracy have never understood, for they always confuse equality with similarity. When it is said that men are equal before the law, the meaning is not that men are equally wise or equally just; and when political equality is claimed, it is not implied that all citizens have equal political knowledge. So here in regard to taste and the power to indulge taste; if all have a more equal power, it does not follow that the taste of each will be equally good or even that those who have good taste will have the same taste.

No sensible man desires an exact equality of income among all the members of a community; for all sensible men prefer that there should be differences of income in different households. Indeed, there is a sort of pride in being less wealthy than one's friends—pride partly because one's friends who are more wealthy show by their friendship that it is not one's power to give which makes them friends. One is proud to know that one's friends are good friends. But there is a pride also in having less than others and yet using what one has with such skill that no one would suspect it. That is similar to the pride of an artist who can show as fine effects in black-and-white as another can show in colour. It follows that it is desirable to have in a community diversities of income; and indeed in a civilized community there will always be some who choose to be poor, not because they are lazy or too incompetent to be paid well, but because they want something which cannot be had except through poverty. Here, however, we speak of chosen poverty, not of grinding, degrading want among those who lack the bare means to live. One of the greatest evils of the industrial system is that it has degraded the very meaning of poverty so that the conceptions of St. Francis seem ludicrous.

But if we desire an inequality of income, we do not in any sense approve of such inequality as now exists. What is wrong nowadays is not that some have more and some less, but that a few have too much and many too little. The extremes must be abolished without reducing all men's incomes to an exact level. It may be necessary to tax large incomes out of existence and to provide actual "relief" for inadequate incomes; but there may be other and better methods. Our concern here is not with the programme of methods, but with the end in view. That end is quite definitely an egalitarian society in the sense explained above, where all men and women have diversities of income within certain defined limits. Political and economic measures will fix the limits that are possible in any given community; for in one country the limits may be farther apart than in another. Nowadays the extremes of wealth and poverty in England or in the United States or in parts of South America are much greater than they are in Norway or Holland. The more equal distribution of wealth in the latter countries actually assists the growth of democratic sentiments; and it is from this evidence that we make our conclusions as to the necessity for economic equality. It should be clear, then, that the ideal of an egalitarian society is not an abstract conclusion from abstract principles, but a motive conception arising out of actual experience. We can actually tell from experience that extreme riches and poverty are bad, and that a more equal distribution, within limits less divided than the present extremes, is good.

The gradual approach to greater equality, as we have said, is a problem of political and economic method; but the other and more fundamental problem is that of the change in point of view, for while equalization in fact is proceeding, public opinion can advance to a new position. A community can be egalitarian in its standard of life, while it is still suffering from unhealthy extremes of riches and poverty. But that can only come about by the conquest of the worker's point of view over the old admiration for ostentatious wealth.

The first step is positive—not the abnegation of greater wealth, but the fuller use of less wealth. The workers must learn to express themselves in their tastes. They must conquer the old territory of the arts. They must know how to spend what they have before they can convince the whole community that civilization does not depend upon superfluous wealth. Something is already known and felt by manual workers which is not known to the connoisseurs and the art-critics; and that something is essential to a sane appreciation of all the finer aspects of civilized life. That something is the need for energy in self-expression. Indeed, the fine arts cannot exist without blood drawn from the "useful" arts, and there is more to be learnt about painting from the handling of a lathe than from the reading of art-criticism. The same vitality which goes to make the worker's pride in his craft gives him the possibility of using finely the resources at his disposal. The worker's point of view should imply a fuller use of the simplest means of adornment and joyous companionship.

On the other hand, no sensible man imagines that the tastes of the majority of workers is good. Even those among the workers who have the true worker's point of view are not skilled in æsthetic choice. This inability is greater or less in different countries, but in Great Britain our defects are very great, perhaps largely because of external influences of climate or historic development. Contrast the public life of a French or Italian city with that of London or Glasgow. In Great Britain the worker finds some of his tastes, not only in drink but in companionship, supplied by the public-house. Beer and tobacco are "goods"—even in the moral sense of that word; and that they are economic "goods" is proved by the amount one has to pay for bad kinds of them. The worker goes willingly and rightly to the public-house, but that is a sign of defective taste because of the crudity of the civilization there possible. Thick smells of sawdust, of half-empty glasses, and of half-finished pipes obfuscate the mind. One is within closed doors, in a mass, uncomfortably leaning on wood or on one's fellow-man. But in the cafés of France and Italy one may sit at ease even in the poorer quarters, in fresh air, with one's own family. There the life is public in the best sense. The actual contrast in this detail should not mislead us into supposing that Great Britain is in other ways less advanced in civilization; but such observation of ordinary life must be the basis of our judgment on the real taste of the workers. We say, then, that it is in many ways defective. In the choice of entertainments, the decoration of rooms, the wearing of clothes, the methods of companionship, even the best workers are unimaginative—as are the "upper" classes, who have less excuse than the workers.

The new civilization, being based upon a greater equality of economic power, will allow much greater variety in houses, clothes, food, and the production and enjoyment of the fine arts. This variety will follow from the fact that a far greater number of men and women will be free to exercise their choice. Of course, if they are uneducated they will be imitative and the herd-mind will dominate; but it is not inevitable that the taste of a democratic community should be monotonous. Indeed, much of the present imitativeness which prevents variety in the manner of life is due to that false standard of admiration for wealth which we are proposing to destroy.

A popular culture has been in history and may be again the natural setting for the dance, for music, colour, the sense of form and, above all, that ease of contact between persons which a caste-system obstructs. All this is the real civilization. This can be produced in a community dominated by the worker's outlook. Men will be more skilful in the use of limited means; they will be freer to express their own likes and dislikes in their choice and, above all, the growth of civilization will be more rapid than any increase in the mere mechanisms of life can make it. There is no question of Utopia. We are not here speaking of a far-off time in which new standards will be operative; for although it may be long before this new standard dominates the life of the whole world, it may dominate the life of any man who chooses it to-day.

VI

RICHES

SIMPLICITY of private life and more equal power over wealth distributed among all the members of society—these do not imply the impoverishment of civilization. Indeed we assert that wealth is altogether good, and the more of it the better; but the amount of available wealth has no bearing upon the private possession of that wealth. Riches are good, if we mean by riches the power to use the resources of civilization; riches are bad, if we mean by riches the power to prevent others using these resources. It is quite possible that a more civilized society of persons more equal in wealth would also be a society with much more wealth available for common use. We do not, then, in condemning the private possession of exceptional wealth, condemn wealth itself. Certainly the workers in their condemnation of the private control of capital, which is called capitalism, have never made the mistake of condemning capital itself.

Confusions, however, arise in the contrast between persons which may mislead the mind into blind alleys.

The discontent of our time is often expressed in denunciations of the rich. The legitimate complaints of the poor against the limitations imposed on them by their poverty are turned into attacks upon those who do not suffer any such limitations. Thus a legitimate grievance is confused with an unnatural jealousy. This is the battle of the "have-nots" against the "haves," in which the have-nots appear to desire nothing better than to be in the position of those whom they dislike. Thus it is not the private possession of wealth which is opposed, but the fact that others have it: and this form of indignation is not uncommon when other kinds of hostility prevail. For example, in war opponents commonly object to the cruelties of the other side, not because they are cruelties, but because the other side does them. Few are able to feel the same indignation against the bombing of towns by their own side as they feel when they are bombed themselves. Even those who lack wealth therefore must cease to desire wealth as a private possession before they condemn the rich.

Here, however, it will be maintained that there is nothing wrong with riches. The rich are not to be condemned because they are rich. It is desirable to have the use of riches; in this at least both the rich and the poor who complain against them appear to agree. Of course it is not so desirable to be rich that one must sacrifice either intelligence or emotion —still less other people's lives—in order to attain to it. But in its proper place among desires, the desire to be rich is right. The moralists who deny this are entirely wrong; they are probably misled by the lack of vitality which affects some thinkers, and they make a gospel of their own defective energy. But morally it is good to enjoy and to expand the personality by the exercise of power; and riches are a means to to do that.

No doubt there are peculiar difficulties in the private

possession of exceptional wealth ; but to confuse that fact with the use of riches is simply a mistake in reasoning or observation of facts, just as one may confuse being bookish with being wise by implying that education depends upon books. The difficulties in private possession arise in the process of becoming rich ; for "the ways to enrich are many, most of them foul," and some become rich by accident, which is not either right or wrong. Also the superfluity of means obscures the importance of the end ; and the rich therefore find it difficult to use well what they have. Clearly they must find it difficult, or their use of it would not be so bad as it is ; and it is more polite to suppose that their defective civilization is due rather to ignorance than to ill-will. Perhaps they and the majority who are their admirers do not yet recognize how feebly and barbarously the rich use their wealth. No need to refer to the primitive barbarism of the few who go to Monte Carlo or Deauville. Indignation is wasted upon such stupidity. Astonishment is excusable. But look at the dress and houses of the majority of the rich : some indeed hire taste, some ape it; the majority frankly ignore it. Quite apart, therefore, from the evil consequences of a reckless expenditure, the futility of what most of the rich enjoy is proof that it is difficult to be rich *rightly* ; but it is not a proof that there is anything wrong with riches. It must not be imagined, then, that all is well with the rich— we say only that being rich is, in itself, good. But in what way good ?

First, it is good for us all, even for those who walk, that some should ride : and if one man goes fast and far in the most perfect mechanism, or if he goes in hitherto untried comfort, and not in a mediæval cart or a nineteenth-century railway carriage, that is all to the good. It is quite irrelevant for anyone to say it would be better if *he* went in comfort, and not his neighbour. It is not necessarily better; and no man is likely to be a just judge in his own case. Quite possibly it is better for all of us that Smith, who now goes in a car, should continue to go, and not give place to Jones. In any case we refuse to take Jones's opinion on the point.

Secondly, it is good that there should be available in a civilized society, for all to use, the widest spaces, the most excellent roads and the noblest buildings. A community of those who live simply in private must be also a community able to live grandly in public. What is good in riches, then, is what may be held in common; and here again we need not refer for proof to any abstract theory, for we have as proof the experience of recent times. There are already public roads, public parks, public buildings, libraries, picture-galleries and theatres, which are as far superior to the possession of the ancient aristocracy as these were better than the wilderness. The worker's view of life involves the highest appreciation of all that is available through economic power; and policy must therefore be such as to preserve and increase available riches by destroying the limitations now set to their expansion. Private possession of exceptional wealth is bad because it does not permit wealth itself to grow; but we have already found another way.

Collections of great paintings which are now a common possession were first made by rich men. The National Gallery in London has grown out of the collection of Mr. Angerstein, and the British

Museum began with the collections of Sir Robert Cotton and Sir Hans Sloane.

But not only the arts and the sciences, even the common resources of ordinary men to-day were once the experiments of the rich. The clothing which most of us in industrial areas now use is the achievement of past fashion. It is not without defects; but in Greece and the Middle Ages the majority wore only one filthy long-lasting cover to their skin. The workers of mediæval England went almost bare, not by choice, but by necessity; and probably the ancient Greeks and Romans would have been more comfortable if more clothing had been available. We are, no doubt, overclothed nowadays; for, as it will be said elsewhere, the body is disgraced in modern cities. But that is no reason to be sentimentally naked in winter. The Greeks did not like it. Nor did our mediæval ancestors. But in those days warm clothing was the privilege of the rich, and they found it so good that others have now contrived to get it. As for food, the spices which seasoned the dreadful meat of the Middle Ages came at great expense from the East. The poor then died or suffered from diseases due to bad food; but the rich were experimenting. Pepper and salt are now not only for rich men's feasting, and in most industrial countries the fruit and even the daily bread comes from lands much more distant than those which sent spices to Europe in the Middle Ages.

In our houses too we have chimneys now which once were only in the halls of the rich. The mediæval hut of mud and wattle without windows—with a hole in the roof for the wandering smoke of a wood fire, if the family could afford it—these were the conditions of the serfs; and the craftsmen fared little better. Even the rich then had little enough warmth from their huge fireplaces, and quite enough dirt among the rushes of their floors. As for light, the majority had none and the rich only stinking candles. The wealthiest burgher of mediæval Florence would be astonished to see the electric light and the stove of some villager in the country round Florence to-day.

The great staircases and rooms of Renaissance palaces are first experiments which may be useful when we come to build the great halls of our future schools, academies or councils. The soaring skill of Tintoretto and Veronese gave to the rich of their day the first hints of the decoration which in the future all may share. Thus, historically, civilization owes much to the rich, which many not rich have now inherited. But lest we should make the mistake of supposing that civilization consists of riches, we must reckon our available power which has not come from the increase in the supply of commodities. If we owe a debt to the rich for the expansion of our civilization, it may seem that the poor are without heirs. Those miserable many in past ages who have suffered and have striven against strait circumstance may seem to have suffered and fought in vain. They were not able to be all that they had it in them to be, and thus died without having lived. They inherited little enough. They may seem to have left nothing. But here one comes upon one of the deeper currents of human life. To the superficial glance nothing appears in the pageant of history but the glitter of the surface—the pomp of kings. Who cares for the half-starved crowd, except that they raise a nameless cheer to see the kings passing? Yet historians are beginning to feel, at least vaguely, that we are the heirs of that crowd. How the common man lives is obviously important both as an explanation of the present and as one of the chief influences upon the future; and here we must include even the very poorest of those common men—the fringe of civilization, those who seem to have derived no benefit from the society in the midst of which they lived. What have they had to give?

A rich man lying in pain among all the resources of his wealth is poor enough. He cries like a poor man. He dies as well or as badly. But suppose that the doctor helps him to recover; the doctor comes with all the knowledge of the body available after centuries of experiment and observation, and he gives more than riches.

The colleges of our Universities were the houses of poor students. The Sorbonne, Trinity College in Cambridge, New College in Oxford, were made what they have been by the poor, for the gifts of the founders are as nothing compared with the common life and learning there contributed by the poor. In England the rich have seized the benefits of the tradition ennobled by the poor; but poor "Clerks of Oxenford" created the tradition of learning and culture to which the workers of to-day are the legitimate heirs.

It is, of course, folly to identify the poor with the manual workers, for there is no essential connection between labour and want except in a barbaric or slavish society. But undoubtedly it is from the worker's point of view that the contribution of the poor is best seen. The workers know that the value of what has been done to build up civilization has been largely contributed by the energy of men. The workers know that the gifts of rich men did not build the cathedrals, but the hands of poor men. The walls of the oldest or the newest houses have in them the life of those hands which was expended in building them; and those hands were poor.

But the poor have something else to give—a philosophy of life. There is a story that one of the early Franciscans, coming out of a church, was offered alms by a rich woman but graciously refused to accept. She then said: "But the poor receive"; to which he replied: "Lady, I have *chosen* to be poor." In the age of economic science the social value of poverty could not be perceived, because no one was willingly poor. But a person with great vitality, able to admire riches and the appetite for riches, may nevertheless choose to be poor. He will not, of course, choose dirt or starvation or disease; but he may choose to give very little, if any, attention to providing himself with goods and services. He may be poor for the sake of freedom and being poor thus he performs a great social service. Indeed, it may be that we need to be reminded that a poorer England may be a happier England. At any rate the poor are able to show personality without its trappings. The rich give their belongings, but the poor give themselves: it is a more magnificent gift. The place which the poor have filled in history, however, must not be made a justification for sentimentalism about poverty. We have assumed that wealth is good for everyone; and it follows that a civilized society would not endure the existence in its midst of the thousands who are now without enough food or clothing or space to live in. We hide away the evils we have not attempted to cure. The Emperor Augustus built a wall to prevent the slums of the Suburra being seen from his new Forum, and the Renaissance Popes built a screen of pillars round St. Peter's to hide the slums of the Borgo. So we now segregate the starving. But there must be no starving; it is not enough for civilization to forget them. All men must share the available wealth.

At present there are two classes of those who are starved to death. There are in any country where unemployment is endemic great numbers of men, women and children who could use their arms and their brains to add to the common store of wealth, but they are prevented by the hesitation to reorganize society. There is no possible reason, except the incompetence of men, why these men, women and children should not have enough to eat and enough to do. But there is another class of poor who are really incapable of adding to the common store of intelligence or wealth. These are the wreckage of malorganization in the past; and the tragedy of to-day is that we are increasing their number by the continuance of obsolete methods of industry and government. Education has been more general in many countries in the recent past, but there are still thousands of adults in contemporary society who did not have education or had so little as to be mentally incapable. Industry has increased our supplies, but there are still thousands who have not obtained any more than crumbs from the full tables of our great cities.

Worse still, great numbers of those whose daily work provides them with the bare means of living have no resources to protect them from falling by accident into the ranks of the poor. The railwayman who has all his life helped forward the commerce and intercourse of civilization is compelled to retire at sixty-five with a miserable pittance to which hard-won savings from a bare livelihood may, with good fortune in health, have been added. It may seem, therefore, a long way to go before we reach even that simplicity which we have discussed as an ideal; for that simplicity at least implies an adequate supply given to each member of a community.

But the worker's resolution to amend the paltry civilization of to-day does not thus confine itself. We do not expect a mere pittance. The poverty of the present must be altogether abolished; and we shall have as well such great resources for knowledge and pleasure that the civilization of the past will be seen to be only a childish beginning.

The worker's view reconciles an admiration for increasing economic power with a respect for virtues which hitherto have been found chiefly among the poor; for it should not be assumed that in abolishing poverty we shall give no place to the old virtues of carelessness in regard to riches. The world of the workers is not to be rendered only or chiefly in terms of wealth. This is fundamental; for the danger of admiration for power is that it may cause forgetfulness of what is greater. The obsession with wealth, even public wealth, may lead to an externalism in which the soul of man is dissipated by trivialities. A community with the best possible railways and banks, all socialized, may be a community of mean spirits; the increase in the instrument of civilization may exhaust the mind in externals so that the inner life is left a barren desert. As a reminder of that danger, therefore, it is well to contrast the shallow wit of some of the wealthiest industrial districts with the high intelligence and fine emotions of poorer peoples living close to nature. Civilization does not consist of possessions or powers, but of subtlety and vigour in body and mind; and this may be had with few or many possessions, only on condition that men's minds are full and strong. The free mind uses wealth or neglects it with equal ease.

VII

ECONOMIC OBSTACLES TO FREEDOM

The worker who is conscious of the social value of his work, who takes a new attitude towards his own enjoyments and the riches which should be available for all, is faced by hindrances and obstacles. The very expansion of his own personality makes him aware of what lies in his way. He sees round him inherited evils preventing the growth of the civilization of which he is the guardian; but some of what is evil is already so obsolete as to be decayed. Traditional superstitions and admirations are expiring. There remains, however, one great obstacle. It is the economic system of the industrial era.

All suggestions for improving civilization are idle rhetoric unless they include a policy for the treatment of industry, commerce and, above all, finance. It is not necessary here to draft Bills for the reform of the existing practices; but we must make out the chief features of the industrial life of the civilization we desire, for men cannot dance or dress finely without bread to eat or shelter in which to sleep. A living wage and a decent home to live in are indeed minor matters by comparison with the other goods which the workers desire; but these at least they must have—for without these their freedom is restricted as by prison quarters and worse than prison fare. No man is free who cannot by willing effort get enough to eat or find a good place to live in. A man marooned on an inhospitable rock is as free as that. But great numbers in our midst, with an appetite for life and its good things as keen as the keenest, are thus imprisoned by the mere structure of our industrial and financial system, and starved by its inadequate provisions for their needs.

Before describing a better state, we must define exactly the present evil. What are the economic chains by which men are now bound ? What is it in the industrial or financial system which restricts liberty ?

First, there is poverty, which is as irreconcilable with civilization as disease or crime ; but the efforts to make it impossible have not yet been more than childish. It is not even generally recognized that more than twenty adults out of every hundred in industrial actions die of semi-starvation and of inadequate clothing and shelter. The immense waste should convict industrialism of incompetence ; for these men and women have hardly lived before they die. Obviously, then, they have no freedom at all. But above the so-called "poverty-line" there are millions of workers in all lands, not only under industrialism, who have no share in the available music, painting or literature, not to speak of the parks and palaces of civilization. It will hardly be maintained that anyone else would lose if poor men were able to hear music and see painting ; but the rich are so much afraid lest their money be distributed that they are hardly willing to consider the distribution of other forms of wealth. Perhaps it is a dangerous concession that poor men are allowed to use the roads ! However, they clearly are not free when the best that civilization has is forbidden to them by what is called " price "—another name for the will of the rich.

With poverty or lack of adequate economic power for bare life we must connect the lack of economic security from which great numbers suffer. The newspapers do not ordinarily give any impression of disasters which may fall upon thousands of working-class houses for no other reason than a change in the weather or the caprice of taste a thousand miles away. But here is a note of the *Daily Telegraph* of October 25, 1924, under the heading " More Miners under Notice ": " Owing to the continued acute depression in the coal trade, the directors of the Cramlington Coal Co., Northumberland, have reluctantly decided to give notice to 2,000 men and boys at their Dudley, Hartlepool and Lamb pits to terminate work fourteen days from this week-end." This indicates distress for 2,000 persons and their dependents; but which 2,000 out of the whole number of workers in those pits? The decision which shall suffer is not made with any reference to need or ability; for it means only that any 2,000 names by pure chance are struck off the wage-sheets. And this again involves that even those who do not actually happen to suffer from unemployment live in a continual danger that their names may be among the unlucky. This is barbarism, not civilization. It is chaos, not organization. But those who suffer do not yet know their own strength and power to change the system.

The second great obstacle to freedom is riches. The expenditure of the rich directs production into socially trivial channels, while the needs of civilization are not supplied. For example, the price of a diamond or a fantastic dress, or the seventh motor-car of a millionaire, induces the supply of these for one man, while thousands cannot with their pence make their need for bread into any effectual demand. We have already allowed for the social utility of rare luxuries and elaborate amenities—as experiments looking towards the future; but that does not justify the gluttony of any man or the waste upon what cannot be used. Great numbers of domestic servants or wide acres waste for sport are instances of the same evil in riches; and all such conditions take the blood out of the veins of civilization and thus prevent liberty. The available supply of services for extending liberty is restricted because of the absorption of these services by the rich. The amount so wasted may not amount to much statistically; but this "set" towards rich men's caprice disturbs the whole current of credit for production.

Thirdly, freedom is limited because so small a proportion of the wealth of any community is common wealth as contrasted with private wealth. In concrete terms we have roads and water as common wealth, but shelter and space and the dignities and the finer amenities of life are held privately. No one wants everything in common, and the proper division of public and private wealth is a matter for experiment. But clearly our civilization can afford to extend considerably the common wealth in order to increase freedom. Take for example the common wealth in knowledge or good taste, which is supposed to be distributed in education: we must think of the process of distribution in terms of rooms and walls and the apparatus of books and desks, besides the number of teachers. But so considered, clearly knowledge is not distributed generally through a sufficiently long period in the life of the new generation; and the usual excuse is that we cannot " afford " it. As well might we say that we cannot afford clothes or drains : but in any case the present system limits freedom, for education is a method of allowing the inner forces to expand into new fields and without education such forces are cramped or wither utterly and die. The fact that public expenditure on education is so very small is a restriction of liberty. The expanding minds of the new generation are hampered by the economic need for earning a living or the absence of sufficient provision to feed their minds on knowledge and fine emotions.

Again, the public wealth is wrongly distributed. The kind of goods and services which most civilized communities enjoy in common are not in the main those goods and services which are productive ; for example, the available funds of all civilized governments are largely wasted on armaments. Of course armaments are necessary ; but in the same way splints or crutches are necessary—so long as men are so uncivilized as to be unable to devise political machinery for the adjustment of national or governmental rivalries. But so long as great amounts of wealth are spent upon mere crutches or primitive needs, so long is freedom restricted by the lack of wealth for other uses. Social welfare, health, education, justice and civil administration, must all be limited by the need to spend upon armaments.

These restrictions on freedom are largely the results of the present economic system, which is itself the result of certain dominant impulses and desires. The system itself is natural and inevitable in so far as it follows necessarily from the domination of certain impulses in the relationships of men ; but it is by no means inevitable and, in one sense, it is not " natural " that these impulses should dominate. Some have said that the dominant impulse is the acquisitive which thus obstructs the creative; but that is probably bad psychology, for the acquisitive is part of the creative impulse, and in any case it does not explain the chief characteristics of industrial civilization. The fundamental fact is separatism of individuals. The two impulses which may be contrasted are the associative and the segregative; for the nineteenth century has in economic matters largely tended to emphasize the impulses and tendencies which divide men.

Specialization and concentration upon specific limited interests have been the characteristics of the past century—not only in the economic sphere; and the existing economic system in industrial nations gives every advantage to the impulse towards selfishness and opposition to others. It is not denied that some good has come out of this impulse. A sturdy independence and vigour does come out of fighting. The "warre of each against all" has accidental advantages; but its main result, as Hobbes said, is a life that is "nasty, brutish and short." Even if some good, however, has come from unlimited competition, few deny now that the balance between competition and co-operation in the life of society must be weighted in favour of co-operation. Competition, in fact, limits freedom; co-operation increases it, since the sphere of power for each man co-operating with his fellows extends into the acts of his fellows, but in competition the power of each is limited by the power of the other. Apply this principle to production and consumption, and it follows that the way to increase freedom is to socialize the organization of industry. It does not follow, of course, that every form of industry should be organized by the State or through the legislature. Some industries may be best so organized; but there are many different possible ways of socializing services, and all must be treated experimentally. The risk of radical attempts is no greater than the risk we run if we make no attempt at all to organize our industrial services more intelligently than they are organized at present.

The governing principle implies, first, that industry should be organized, as government is, upon the basis of public service. Most men in any state of society will think naturally at first of what gain they or their families may derive from the rendering of any service, and this not because men are selfish, but because the effect upon themselves is the most definite effect of their service which they can understand. But that need not involve the continuance of the present domination of the appetite for private gain. Society can allow for the private interest of each and yet enforce the consideration by each of the common needs of all. Such enforcement may be by methods of organization or by the pressure of new customs and beliefs; and as men become more civilized, more men will naturally begin to feel that their occupations are primarily social services, although inevitably sources of income for themselves. To begin that transformation in the economic system is in the power of every man even to-day. We have too little appreciation of what individual change of attitude and conduct can do: we tend to look too continuously for action by or through social units. On the other hand, the fundamental change must be made socially. Our principle involves that all industry, whether "nationalized" or not, shall be dominated by the needs for public service. This must be embodied in law, administration and industrial organization. No production or consumption should be possible except mainly for the sake of public service, and always under conditions favourable to that service. Thirdly, therefore, all industrial organization must be "democratic" in the sense that the servants of the public in industry are free. This implies "control by the workers"; and that phrase must be understood to mean the power to decide on hours, conditions and security of tenure by the workers, as well as a share for them in the power to fix wage-rates. It is also implied in free service or in "control by the workers" that, as there is mental as well as manual work to be done by all workers, they should play an organic part in the direction and management of enterprises. Freedom does not involve domination of the whole situation, although it must involve having power to work with one's brain as well as with one's hands.

But, after all, it is not industry but finance which imprisons the world at present. The organizers of industry, commonly called employers, are in fact in the same prison with the workers; for their best efforts are often thwarted by the quite different activities of the financiers. In one sense the interests of employers and employed *are* the same; that is to say, they are both opposed by the interest in money, irrespective of its source or its use, which is the dominant interest of financiers.

Let us not, however, imagine that financiers and bankers are wicked, unnatural parasites upon the otherwise kindly human race. They are parts of a system, and the system lives upon the ignorance and selfishness which is to be found in all classes. The financiers carry out, perhaps efficiently (but even that is doubtful), a system which they did not create, which they maintain only because it needs them. The essence of that system is the assumption that *what is most highly paid for is best worth doing*; and every man maintains that system who thinks of his occupation or his possessions as the source of his income without reference to the service that occupation or property performs. The same false assumption involves that no reference is made to the well-being or the injury which is the result of the production or use of goods. In many cases it may be difficult to calculate the amount of good and evil in such a result; but in some cases it can hardly be said to be doubtful. For example, wheat is clearly more useful than pearls; and *in a state of society such as now exists* more wheat is needed and fewer pearls. If all men had food, then pearls might be a public good; but while some men starve, the utility of pearls must be largely private. How much private good must be sacrificed to public need is doubtful; but we all agree that some such sacrifice should be made.

No reference, however, is made to all this when the profit on an investment is in question. There are, indeed, some investments which bring large profits—such as the maintenance of brothels and gaming houses—which are morally condemned and legally forbidden; but over a large field no attempt is made to consider what investment yields most public good. The moral problem of the individual investor is not our concern here; for we are more concerned with *the control of credit.* The bankers and financiers give credit to industrialists and salesmen, having in mind the rate or the security of their profit, but *not* having regard to public need for the service which the issue of credit makes possible. A banker, indeed, has no competence in estimating social results; for the system prevents his having any other purpose in his mind except the rate of profit on the credit. Similarly the financier has in mind no other use of invested capital except its earning capacity. It is not denied that the rate of profit on investment is a sign of what the public wants; nor is it denied that in a wholly civilized community the public wants only what it needs. It is, indeed, never safe to say that one man, however wise, knows what another man needs.

On the other hand, as against individualism, it is true that sometimes the onlooker sees most of the game. If the sense of public need is external to the mind of the majority, if it is the peculiar possession of a segregate caste, then organization based upon that sense is tyrannical. But it is not inevitable or natural that the sense of public need should be restricted to a few. The greater number in a civilized community may acquire and develop such a sense; and indeed it has been so developed among a whole community in all the great periods of civilization. Even in the industrial period this sense has proved to be operative in the maintenance of nationality, for men have died in war for what they believed to be a common good.

It may become operative in the daily life of business, in work in the factory and the counting-house. As that sense of public need increases in effectiveness, it will become clearer; and the principles according to which we may judge this or that investment or issue of credit will become easier to apply.

Freedom requires that the investment of capital, privately or publicly owned, and the issue of credit shall be socialized; that is to say, the dominant motive should be the *public need*, the supply of which is made possible by such investment or issue of credit. The method by which this can be achieved will not be discussed here. Perhaps when "nationalization of the banks" is advocated this is what is intended; but perhaps more varied and more subtle measures are necessary for the direction of credit into public channels. It may be that even at present some bankers and financiers have in mind the public need; but if so, they must be incompetent or ineffectual, for in fact the public need is not served. It is plainly nonsense to say that we cannot have enough houses and clothes and food, or that we cannot "afford" such goods for every man. It is mainly a question of credit—putting aside the possible incompetence of our organizers of production and sale. A State-issued or State-guaranteed credit for a million houses would make a very productive return in mere wealth in ten years' time. Of course it would ruin some few who are now supplying houses on the profit basis: but it is difficult to see why they should not be ruined, since others are killed in war or starved in peace.

All this new system of organizing production and finance will be for the advantage of the workers; that is to say, chiefly for the advantage of the wage-earners but also for the advantage of all who take part in production. But this interest in the fortunes of the workers is not a "class" interest. It is not in opposition to the interests of any group within the community which has anything of its own to add to the common life. Only parasites are excluded by a policy based upon the worker's point of view. All others must necessarily derive benefit from such a policy.

This, however, is not said merely to soothe ruffled feelings or to destroy the thrill of old women in drawing-rooms and clubs who enjoy the sensation of expecting a bloody revolution. By all means let them expect the worst! Again, no claim is made that all men and women should feel that their chief interest is served by manual labour. Feelings differ and the estimates of what is valuable should always be changing. The main point of the argument is that the interest of the workers is *necessarily* an interest in the whole community and cannot be a class interest because it aims at the release and development of all those human forces which contribute to the life of the whole. Here is a navvy ill-housed, uneducated and unskilful: to give him a good education and a good house is, no doubt, a worker's policy, but it is not a "class" policy. The efficiency and happiness which thus increases in him accrues to the whole community.

On the other hand, the need of the workers should not lead them to have no thought for others. Policy must not be based upon gaining advantage for those who suffer wrong except on the assumption that all may gain.

It is sometimes argued that one cannot afford to be generous. On that ground we must trick the grocer in case the grocer should trick us. But the worker's point of view is certainly full of generosity. The workers are not likely, unless deluded by demagogues, to forget the interests of others. They can support fundamental change without any hostility to those who may have to suffer when they gain; for it is not a choice between two opposing camps. It is not a question who shall lose; for as long as the workers feel that their gain can only be measured in loss to the employers, so long will the minds of men be chaotic and their schemes inadequate. We must remove the issue on to another plane and calculate, not in terms of gain to this or that element in the community, but in terms of the whole community. We do not say that no one will lose; but we do say that what they lose will be more than compensated by what they gain. A man and a community may well sacrifice wealth for freedom; and the only freedom which can be preserved is that which is shared by all the members of the community.

VIII

PATRIOTISM

FREEDOM must be won by each man first in his own country, for that is the part of the world which is most nearly himself. Every man has somewhere in him a memory of childhood, and even a poor or sickly child has had moments of delight which survive the rest of experience. Every man looks back to some place or some dear persons who were the familiar setting within which he first became conscious of himself. For some the memory of scenes familiar in childhood remains vivid; for others these scenes remain only in a half-conscious discomfort when the depths of their souls are stirred. But all have the roots of their being twisted about the earth and the simple circumstances of their earliest life; and the sap from such roots is patriotism.

Again, apart from memory, every man has a natural attachment to what is taken for granted as the basis for his daily life. The traditional language, the current customs, become part of one's self; and so do the persons whose life in common with us is the sole reason for language and custom. Thus the individual is on every side protected by the familiar as the sapling in a wood is sheltered from the wind by other trees. The pull of the memories of childhood, combined with that of the familiar daily facts, makes up the force which moves us when "our country" is felt as a reality.

The great majority of any nation feel that pull most intensely when a disturbance of normal life makes them conscious of their need of the familiar. Sometimes the feeling of patriotism has reference to a small group of persons or a small area of hill and valley. Sometimes that feeling includes among its objects millions who, we know, are of our sort and large sections of the earth's surface. Sometimes patriotism is altruistic; sometimes a man feels the importance of his fellows only by reference to his own loss and gain. But the passion itself is widespread and powerful.

Those who mean by their country the wealth and comfort they possess may well desire others to die in their defence; but they need to be reminded that the majority have no share in the benefits their country confers upon them. The patriotism of the rich is, thus, often an insult to the poor; and those who have nothing to lose may well revile those who call upon them to protect what is valuable.

But those are wrong who say that the oppressed have no country. It is true that the great majority have little of the best that any country contains. The land is not theirs: they have no share in its wealth, and little enough of liberty even in England, for a man is not free who may die unchained but cannot move from the place in which he was born or choose any of the goods he sees. It may seem that the dispossessed have little to lose from foreign conquest, and have no real interest in defending what others possess. But the majority—who are handworkers and are poor—know better than the theorists that their country is not the wealth and the power which others control. The shepherd, the coal-miner, the textile worker and the seaman, know an England that is not in the textbooks of economics nor in the drawing-rooms of the rich. That England is in the earth on the downs or in the stern valleys where coal lies hid or in the mists or on the stormy coasts; but more truly it is in the common speech and the dear habits of equals known familiarly. That England is not a heap of wealth or a system of government, but a common life to which our own life is felt to be tributary. We working men make that England and that is why we are willing to die for it, not in order to get something out of it nor in order to keep what little we have. That England is flesh of our flesh as the child is made of the father. It is for what we give to it, and not for what we get out of it, that it is dear to us; and the mere balance of advantage and disadvantage which a poor man may derive from his country is irrelevant where his affections are concerned. Indeed, even the most oppressed never casts such accounts of profit and loss when an appeal is made in the name of his country. There is a service which is not rendered for payment and that the workers give for what they know as England. They take no credit for their giving. They *are* England.

This is not the service of a myth or a fetish. The majority are not misled in this. Of course they may take many false cries for the true voice of England. They may fight and die for what destroys or disgraces the country they love. They may be fooled or they may be culpably blind. But the possibility of being mistaken does not prove that their emotion itself is futile, as sentimentalism does not prove the love of a person to be foolish. There may be worthy objects of love. The capacity for loving one's country, indeed, is altogether admirable, and more countries are worth loving than may seem to be at first sight. Cynics never see what is fundamental, however correct their perception may be of the many errors which lie upon the surface of public life; but the fear that patriotism may mislead is an ungenerous prudence which is commoner among an intellectual caste than among manual workers.

What then is this country which is worthy of love? We have said already that it is not a mass of wealth: it may, however, be imagined that it is the power which dominates. Especially in those nations which have an empire over others, it is difficult for the common man to avoid admiration of power. He feels himself exalted by the sense that men of his race control other races; and the weakling child of a city slum may feel unnatural pride when he hears of Englishmen bombing the stalwart Arabs or the scholars of China, for the weakling easily admires strength, as the coffee-house poet of the eighteenth century admired the country life. The simplest patriotism is barbaric. The tradition of the schools inculcates this barbaric patriotism, for school history is generally the uncritical acceptance of records and moral judgments of our more primitive ancestors. The greater historians, of course, are able to lift the record on to another plane where it can be judged by reference to the moral standards of civilized man; but the nations still preserve in their schools and in their popular tradition the hostility to foreigners and the belief in war as a successful method of dealing with them. Even this crudity is not without some justification, for most nations have had to fight for their existence. The defect of the tradition is that it omits to notice the great gains derived from foreigners and the good done by men of our own race in their intercourse with foreigners. The wars of the past do not explain the civilization of the present, for the whole of civilized life in any nation is a product of the intercourse of many peoples. As a Swedish poet has said: "Nothing is completely national—except barbarism."

The past which has been so full of wars is also full of the records of the simpler forms of heroism which arise in war. National heroes are generally warriors. Among the monuments to great men in any city the majority are monuments to generals and admirals; and in the old-fashioned history the rank and file, who were in fact the workers, have little honour. Our country in such terms as these is the country of a few important men. But a transformation has been worked under the eyes of this generation. Even the victories of war have been placed to the credit of the nameless dead who were the craftsmen, the miners, the engine-drivers of peace. The rank and file, and that not of a professional soldiery but of labour, has won and lost in different countries. Between the lines is no man's land, and on either side the workers. The kings of an earlier age are gone; and the generals are watched by sterner eyes—the eyes of men misled. In many civilized countries, too, women have come to consciousness of the need for their thought and their labour—not the ladies of romance who crowned or comforted dukes or barons, but common women, textile workers transformed into munition workers, clerks become nurses, and the many unclassed who filled the place of transport workers. That this discovery of the workers should have been made in a great war does not make it less important or more fruitful for peace: for to those workers who are conscious of what has happened it has brought a sense that peace and war are in their hands. At any rate, patriotism is no longer the following of the titled few; it is the comradeship of nameless common folk.

It is impossible for the workers looking across trenches or frontiers to feel enduring hostility to workers on the other side. The patriotism of the common man must inevitably revise their view of their own country and its relation to others. The labour that keeps each nation alive is too like that of every other nation. The miner knows the mines abroad better than he knows the palaces in his own land, as may be seen by a statement of plain fact which shows what labour means. A British trade-union leader coming one evening from a Yorkshire mine saw the news of a mine disaster in Belgium. He went from his home to the station, and was in Belgium next morning. He found his way to the place of the accident, and saw that the men on the surface were dazed and nothing was being done. He could speak nothing but Yorkshire dialect; but he kicked open a shed, took a lamp and lowered himself into the shaft. At the foot of the shaft he found three boys who had crawled there and he brought them up. Then courage came to the onlookers and in the end fifteen men were rescued. The Britisher is now well known to the workers in many lands; and both he and they have a new idea of England.

Apart from all consciousness of solidarity the mere growth of economic and political organization is making it impossible to regard one's country as it was regarded by former generations. It is not, in fact, the same country, for the man is not the same as the child. In the modern world the material which is used by manual labour in industry is largely foreign. Rubber, cotton and oilseeds come from abroad into Europe and America; and from Europe and America machinery goes to be used by the workers in other lands. Again, the common food and clothing of the workers in industrial countries come largely from abroad. Coffee, tea and meat are not now, as they were in earlier times, reserved by their rarity for the rich. Every worker, then, at least in Western civilization, may see that his own home is largely made up of foreign elements; and all the conscious workers know that England and France are giving to other lands the resources of civilization. The patriotism of the past, then, is transformed.

No less pride, no less exaltation, and no less affection is derived from the sight of an England which has given and will give the resources of life to the world at large. That England is as real as the conquering and wealth-acquiring England; but it may need a new focus of our eyes to see it. The history of England would read very differently if historians had looked at other facts than those which first attracted the primitive story-tellers; for there is enough to be found in the records of the past to show both the indebtedness of other nations to England and the debt of England. For example, the English are late-comers in civilization, but already they have introduced many political ideas and scientific or quasi-scientific ideas embodied in machinery. The great achievement of the English in organizing their own political life upon an agreed basis can be shown to have entered into the structure of civilization so that all civilized nations now use the English experience. But all this is only a promise of more to be done. As the worker may see in every finished task the basis for a new achievement, so in patriotism the great deeds of the past may be only first essays for a future masterpiece. All nations can feel that sense of their own power to do benefit to others.

Patriotism is not the privilege of great nations, for quite small nations live by the same affection and devotion of their members; but in a small nation men cannot so easily mistake mere power and wealth for what is lovable. Therefore the patriotism of small nations is often less primitive than that of great nations. The people of a small nation have the same sort of memories of childhood and the same attraction for the familiar as those of an empire; but they are not likely to find any value in domination. They naturally expect their status to depend upon their service to others and to civilization as a whole; and since in most small nations all social classes are in closer contact, and the difference of rich and poor is less extreme, small nations will naturally express a point of view less alien to that of the workers than is the spirit of empires. The policy of small nations is naturally the policy of the workers in all countries; for it implies co-operation and interdependence.

All classes and kinds of men can feel that new patriotism which has been described, but to feel thus is easier and more natural for the working classes than for others. This is not a mere idealization of manual labour. Those who work with their hands are more likely to feel the patriotism of service, of giving and not of getting, because their own positions in society can be honoured only on the basis of service. They, therefore, have an advantageous position for seeing the England which has done good to the world. But those who live by owning capital, who have thus, as the phrase goes, "a stake in the country," or even the lawyers and doctors, are much more likely to think of England in the terms of the wealth and power they share. The patriotism of service, then, is peculiarly the patriotism of Labour.

Labour is sometimes said to be unpatriotic. Indignation against the oppressors in our own land, sympathy for the oppressed in other lands, and a suspicion of drum-beating, flag-waving "patriots"— these certainly are characteristics of Labour, and these are unreconcilable with the older and more primitive forms of patriotism. But the criterion of a man's patriotism is not the amount of noise he makes about it. The true quality of an empire is not to be found in the praise of it. Labour knows well enough how to love its own land—"a land," as the old English geographer wrote of England, "full of mirth and of game, and of men well able to mirth and to game; men strong of hand and of tongue, but the hand is more better and more strong than the tongue."

IX

INTERNATIONAL LIFE

It follows from the conception of patriotism analysed above that each nation should view itself as co-operating with others, and that therefore all foreign contacts should be governed by the international mind; that is to say, the common interests of all nations should dominate the separate interests of each, whenever there is opposition between what is separate and what is common. For example, it may be an interest of the people of England taken separately to sell cotton goods in India; but it is a common interest of many nations, including England, that the Indian textile arts should be preserved and developed, and not destroyed by a flood of factory products. On the other hand, it cannot be taken for granted that the textile arts of India must be preserved at all costs. They too may be rightly sacrificed for a common good; and it may be in the end a common good of all nations that industrially produced cotton goods should be used in India. This example will show how difficult it is in some cases to say precisely what policy is best for the common good; but the general principle is not in doubt. In the same way as between individuals, the separate good of each may be more easily seen; but the common good should prevail and an effort must be made to discover what it is.

In commercial or industrial issues our governing ideas are too crude to allow at present any growth of clear international conceptions, for we have not yet escaped from the primitive stage of competition for private gain, much less from competition between national groups for separate wealth. For example, in the organization of a recent international exhibition it was desired to show British wares in a national section; but each British firm refused to allow its products to be shown in any manner that would improve the setting for the products of another British firm. Here not even the national point of view could dominate; and it is still more difficult to reach the international point of view. The interests even of allies are not always common. Nevertheless resolute thinking can and does find definite issues in regard to which the interests of many peoples are the same: health and scientific knowledge are even nowadays admitted to be common international interests, and it is possible that we shall soon think in the same way of finance or the standard of life.

The general principle that co-operation between nations is better than rivalry, aloofness or hostility, is granted by many who in no sense adopt the worker's point of view. The form of co-operation, however, remains to be defined. Clearly, even robbers may co-operate, and many privileged groups in the past have co-operated internationally to maintain their positions. The workers co-operate with a different end in view, and in general their purpose is to secure internationally the organization of freedom for the productive and progressive work of the world. As the richer classes of one nation still look for help to the powerful and the wealthy of another, so the coal-miner looks across his frontier to other coal-miners. That is no lack of the national sense. Indeed, no class is less national by marriage, inheritance or acquisitions than the so-called "upper" class; for the wealthy are often *déracinés* by the very force of their wealth. But no class is more completely national in its characteristics than the manual workers of every country. They have most obviously the defects and the excellences of every nation.

For about a century, however, those who have had the worker's point of view have seen that no group of workers can attain what they want except by action in international life; and in spite of the great difficulties due to language, to the poverty which divides, to the lack of time and energy, the workers have maintained international organizations both in the political and in the industrial sphere.

These organizations are historic facts of the greatest importance—perhaps of more importance than international financial groups or commercial alliances. But we are not here concerned with the description of facts. Tendencies are more significant. The international organizations of the workers indicate that, as political life has been democratized, and as industry must soon cease to be an autocracy, so international life is beginning to feel the will of the common man. It has already become ludicrous to hear the cultured nonentities of diplomacy pretending to teach "foreign affairs" to trade unionists who have shared the lives of common folk abroad. Travel is no longer a privilege of the *jeunesse dorée.* The movement of students from land to land is repeating at a higher level the mediæval internationalism; and there are already many manual workers who have a keener sense of international interests or national differences than professed students of foreign peoples.

Quarrels, of course, may arise between groups of workers from different lands. The interests of such groups may be opposed, as in the case of other national groups. War, therefore, may come in spite of the entry of the workers into active international life. But at any rate the workers will demand reasons. They are not likely to be led passively to slaughter; and the purposes of policy which will appeal to them will be different from those which move the country gentry or the old women in Society. The standard of life of the workers in each country is likely to be a crucial issue for foreign policy. This is not merely a matter of economics; for a comparison of tastes and traditions cannot be rendered in statistics of money value. Japan and China may enter as sellers in the world-market, but their workers may still prefer very simple conditions of life. The rivalries within Europe itself or between Europe and the United States may come to rest upon what the workers want in terms of food and clothing. Big issues are on the horizon, and to the solution of those issues the workers themselves will contribute.

The most important result in politics will be the substitution of a diplomacy of the workers for the diplomacy of property. The oldest type of diplomacy, that of courts and military rivals, has already somewhat receded into the background. It is true that ambassadors can still find kings in some backward nations, and that the forms of politeness, even where there is no king, are generally the forms of the Renaissance court. It is true also that attachés and consuls are still used as military spies by all the great civilized nations; and incomparably foolish these spies seem to be, if their own accounts of their cleverness are true. But in the main modern diplomacy is not concerned with the heads of States or the estimate of rival forces. The far more important modern issues are economic. Diplomacy is now very largely the diplomacy of property; that is to say, its chief concern is the trade or the investments of its nationals in foreign countries. Russia, China, Egypt, Mexico—all these names bring to mind dominant diplomatic issues; and all of these issues turn upon trade and investment. But in recent years the older diplomacy of the "open door" and "most-favoured nation" has become less important than the diplomacy of capital; that is to say, some nations are friendly and others hostile because of the foreign investments of their citizens. There is now a very large amount of the capital of some nations invested under the jurisdictions of other nations. It may be to the advantage of the workers of England, for example, that the capital-owners of England should invest in the Argentine. It may be to the advantage of the workers of France that French peasants' money should be invested by their banks in Roumania. But in any case the advantage accruing to the workers is accidental. It is certainly not a dominant purpose of the investor, nor of the diplomatist or politician who speaks in his name.

The dominance of the worker's view would transform this situation; for the workers' interests would become the dominant purpose of foreign policy. This would require far-reaching changes, because the diplomatist of to-day is generally quite ignorant of the worker's point of view both in his own country and in that in which he resides. Foreign Ministers tend still to think of their function as something too sacred and mysterious to be the concern of the ordinary man; and therefore they tend to forget that the ordinary man should be the first concern of the Foreign Minister. The worker's point of view will, however, inevitably force itself upon the practices and prejudices of diplomacy ; and there may be some consequent disturbance of the dust of the archives.

Secondly, a new international outlook brings into prominence the contrasts of cultures or civilizations. This entirely displaces the petty problems of frontiers and jurisdiction. For example, there is an obvious contrast between the Russian outlook and that of Western Europe and America. This is not the place for analysing these two different views of life and the world ; but clearly it is *not* a contrast between a proletarian or working-class outlook and the attitude of capitalism. The Russian outlook is still very largely what it was under the Tsars. It is no worse for that ; for that means that it is native and national, and not derivative from German theory. But it is alive to-day both in the enthusiasm and in the immense passivity of Russia. It is extremist. It is deeply pessimistic at times, and at other times it is a form of spiritual exultation. Russia has much to give the world under any form of government, but perhaps not in any case a form of government ; for that has *not* hitherto been her strong point.

On the other hand, Western Europe and America are " materialistic " even in their religion. No worse for that, because thereby they keep their feet on the ground and their hand on the plough. But European culture suffers from the obsession of money-making —a meaningless haste ; and it is thoroughly " capitalistic " in the sense that those who live by owning money and not by serving are dominant. Europe, however, is older than capitalism and industrialism. It is the source of many great literatures, of the sciences and of the art of administration. This civilization is now faced with that of Russia; but also with that of the Far East and of Africa. These are the great issues for diplomacy. China and Japan and India and Malaya are not likely to bow down before Europe, still less before any part of it. They have their own arts, their own abilities for the sciences which are not yet fully developed, their own forms of religion and social ideals. The nations of the world may be still so barbaric that differences of outlook will lead them into war; but a skilful diplomacy should find means to make the diverse civilizations co-operate. Again it may be useful to remind ourselves that these civilizations are the products of the present activities, not of a few scholars or of the select rich, but of the body of workers with their hands in the different countries.

Consider, finally, Africa. Even those normally concerned with international affairs do not seem to understand what a vast possibility lies in the African races. There also it will not be a mere bowing before Europe. Too much is known. The Africans of to-day are more likely to believe that Europeans are devils than that they are gods. Guns and gin do not go very well with Christianity, and the attempt to combine them has not made European culture pleasant to Africa. But Africa has her own traditions and by many strange routes they are already beginning to permeate the other types of culture.

Finally, the relation between all nations cannot be, and should not be, exactly similar. Varying extents of intimacy should exist between different nations as between different individuals, for the world of nations is not a collection of similar units. There is an immense difference between Costa Rica and the United States, although it by no means follows that either is worse than the other because it is different. Thus there will naturally arise groups of nations, as, for example, the Scandinavian group.

The nations of the British Commonwealth which are of the same race and tradition are obviously a separate group. The chances of war or of commerce have brought India and parts of the Tropics within the same jurisdiction; and this will naturally form the basis for a real international experiment by which distinct religions and cultures may be preserved in friendly co-operation. This must involve concessions on the part of those who righty complain of past injustices.

The pride of race, however, and the confidence in one's own tradition need not drive one to reject all contact with other races and traditions. These others may have something valuable to give, something which may indeed be essential to the development of one's own country. For example, India and China and Africa have very much to gain from Western science. If "the East" and Africa were to reject these, not only would they be weaker in their influence on the future of the world, but they would limit the development of their own characteristic excellence. Health is as necessary for India as for England and Western science promotes health better than Oriental tradition.

Similarly, for us of the West it is mere cowardice to "cut and run," because some of our influence upon the East and Africa has been pernicious. Europe, having done much wrong as well as much good to other parts of the world, cannot absolve itself from responsibility by simply leaving other continents to their own inhabitants. Our pride, too, is a virtue. We do know more than the East and Africa: and our knowledge gives us certain rights—not, of course, the right to compel, but certainly the right to be heard. Those advocates of subject or undeveloped races who develop a suspicion of their own nation have not sufficient pride even to meet those who have been wronged on other grounds than charity. We must hold out our hand to the East and to Africa with confidence in ourselves, expecting these others to have their own pride as equals.

But one of the immediate dangers of to-day is the alliance between private interests in many nations. The general tendency of the policy of one government may be assisted by other governments. The ruling class or group of "interests" in one country may be supported by similar groups abroad; and on the other hand, revolution in one country may be assisted by sympathy in others. The alignment of policies in opposition may thus be international. But since assistance or sympathy from abroad can always be made to seem adverse to one's own country, each side has a ready weapon against the other in the appeal to patriotism. Thus the Soviet Government was able to gain support in Russia because the Whites used foreign aid, and the Conservative Party in England was able to gain support because their opponents seemed to have the sympathy of Russia. Further, since most governments stand for the established order, the appeal to foreign sympathy is generally made, not by governments, but by their opponents, and therefore internationalism and revolution seem naturally to go together. Finally, this fact leads the opponents of governments to treat most governments or ruling classes as in alliance against them, and therefore makes the conflicting tendencies in all countries more similar. Thus moderate Conservative Governments move closer to reaction and moderate reformers move towards revolution, by the natural gravitation of politics towards definite issues.

International politics makes strange companions. Alliances are formed between tyrannical governments and mild democracies, sympathies are expressed by pacifists for bloodthirsty revolutionaries—and all because opposition to what is near at hand makes it easy to sympathize with what is distant. In the larger issues of rivalry between nations the danger is an over-simplification of policy; for instead of discussing what we must do, it is easier to discover who is our enemy : and thus we may be led into dangerous international hostilities in which the workers of many countries are oppressed by agreement between the capital-owners of those countries. For this reason the attitude towards the present Government in Russia may be crucial, for there is no doubt that agreements of other groups against such a Government may justly be regarded as an obstacle to the liberty of the workers in all countries.

The general body of the manual workers have no natural hostility to foreigners; but as many of them are at present uneducated, they have the natural dislike of what is strange. This dislike is due to a lack of education and not to the fact that they are manual workers; but there is no reason why manual workers should not be as well educated as anyone else, for not everything that is now characteristic of manual workers is essential to manual work. For example, most manual workers speak badly, walk badly, and dress badly, but these are accidents of present circumstance. Similarly, University lecturers generally are incapable of quick action, but that is not an essential accompaniment of learning. The manual workers, then, and workers in general, need to be shown the issues in international politics more clearly. Their friendship for other nations cannot be taken for granted.

It can, however, be shown that co-operation, and not conflict, between nations is the policy which arises inevitably from the worker's attitude towards life. In the first place we need freedom to do our work. War limits freedom; and so does the preparation for war. That is not all: positive co-operation between nations implies opening to each nation new avenues of development—the increase of trade, the development of new resources; and the more of all this there is, the better it is for the workers in a world organized as described above. The workers would soon feel the benefit of developing the resources of foreign countries and tropical dependencies, if such development were not, as it now is, mainly aimed at the enrichment of owners of capital.

The workers also will feel in the development of their own civilization the need for contributions from those of other races and languages. Music, painting, and literature are not reserved for the few. No power can prevent the manual workers from demanding the best of these as well as other goods; and the workers have too acute a sense of facts to be hoodwinked into a cultural protectionism. The increase of civilization by international intercourse in every sphere of human life is therefore essential to the liberty of the workers in all countries.

Finally, from the worker's point of view the great issues of political and economic life are seen to have become international. It is true that each man must secure freedom in his own country first; but even the first steps towards social freedom are hindered by the interlocking of interest and privilege in many different countries. The obstacles to be overcome are international. The instrument to overcome them must therefore be international—as the founders of the workers' internationals knew; but it is still more clear that the force behind the instrument for building a new civilization must be international. The civilization which we have inherited—our arts and sciences, as well as our material resources—are all the results of international intercourse. The labour, therefore, which we now see went to the making of civilized life had its natural outlet in the peaceful and progressive contact between peoples. From the point of view of the workers hostility and war between nations is an obstacle to the effectiveness of labour or an actual waste of labour. It follows that the worker's point of view is naturally and inevitably international, aiming, not at the abolition of nations, but at their co-operation.

Few among the workers of any nation have acquired a new outlook. Ancient superstitions survive in regard to foreigners more easily than they survive in regard to rank or wealth. But the workers quickly respond to the appeal for unity with other workers in every country; and this source of unity is already becoming a force for making the next step in civilization, which is the organization of peace.

X

REFORM AND REVOLUTION

How is the next step to be made? It has been already admitted that the worker's point of view is not yet realized by the majority in any country; still less is it dominant anywhere. A closer approach to making it dominant has been made in some countries than in others; but it is not necessarily more dominant in those countries where theorists more vociferously advocate it. In any case a great change in our present habits would have to occur before international life flowed out of a new patriotism and before the occupations by which men make their living became services rather than exploitation of their neighbours. The method by which such a change could be made may therefore be usefully discussed. It is not a question of the law to be introduced or the vote to be taken; the problem is whether either legislation or voting is powerful enough to bring about such a change as would be implied by the general acceptance of the worker's point of view.

For the sake of making the issue clear, the old contrast between reform and revolution may be used; but it is impossible to compare these two in the abstract or in isolation from the conditions to which they refer. One is not necessarily and in all circumstances better than the other. In the usual sense of the words reform means gradual and limited change, revolution means change which is immediate and fundamental; and no sensible man would say that he advocates either reform or revolution unless he knows to what issues he is referring. It is possible to advocate reform of clothing and revolution in art. The nature of the evil must define the method of cure. The disease must be diagnosed, and the relevant treatment then decided; for it is unlikely that all the evil from which we at present suffer can be cured by one method, even if it be so surgical as revolution.

We should not, however, even discuss revolution unless we thought that some of the evils of to-day were fundamental. If nothing were wrong but a form here and there, a mannerism or an accidental injury, then it would be obvious that radical and rapid measures were uncalled for and even dangerous. But few thinking men to-day would say that the issues in social policy or individual life are trivial. We workers are suffering from a lack of liberty, of education, of fine enjoyments; and thus life is degraded and confused throughout the whole community. That is reason enough for considering whether revolution may be needed.

But there is another reason: even if we do not, others certainly do think existing evils very great and very deeply ingrained in the life of society. And others have acted upon that belief. Revolution is a fact. It has occurred in our own day. We must take account of it as a fact of contemporary life in some countries, and perhaps as a possibility elsewhere.

On the other hand, reform has changed the condition of workers in the factories: it has improved our road system, our education, and our methods of administration. In any normal society reform is a continuous process; and even the most radical revolution would not make reform useless, for no conceivable state of society will be so perfect as to need no improvement. The most violent revolutionary will need to use the methods of reform if he is not to lose all that his revolution may achieve by allowing his gains to become stagnant. Thus the two methods of social change have been used, and can be tested by reference to their results.

The mere matter of fact is not our present interest. The more important issue is the meaning and value of what has occurred and of what may occur in all countries. But in order to understand that issue we must distinguish between external changes and changes of inner tendency or attitude. The two are intimately connected. A woman cannot have her hair bobbed without producing in herself some new emotions; a man cannot grow whiskers and treat the others in his office or workshop in exactly the same way. So also "inner" mental changes may be the results of a mere habit of walking on the left instead of on the right; and revolution does normally introduce external changes of that sort. But the real value and importance of revolution lies in the change of mental "set" or attitude either in individuals or in society, and not in the new external forms; or if in external forms, then only as causes of mental transformation. Thus in Vienna to-day the palaces are without a court or soldiery; but the more important change is in the attitude of the man in the street. The absence of a rich aristocracy in a society is a comparatively trivial fact: far more important is the new sense of equality and pride in their work among the majority of workers, which may be the result of a revolution.

What is the general character of such a change of attitude? That is a problem for social psychology, and we can understand its solution best by reference to the change in an individual's mental or emotional experience. There are two obvious examples of individual transformation—conversion and falling in love. These are not merely changes of direction, as when a man gives up one occupation and takes another, or as when a man believes to be false what he hitherto believed to be true. Changes of opinion are important, but they are not revolutionary. In conversion, on the other hand, the whole colour or tenor of a man's daily actions is transformed. He sees the same trees and houses which he saw before, but, as it were, in a new light. The difference is like that of night and day. He moves in a freer air. Similarly, in that finest example of conversion, when a man throws off theological beliefs and ecclesiastical practices, there is a transformation. The sense of freedom spreads, like the glow of warmth after chill, over the whole person. Body and spirit expand, increase, arise and move upon new paths. The free mind feels its mastery of its inheritance and its own creative power.

Falling in love is another example of transformation. In this case too one feels and acts differently. The world seems entirely different, and the transformation of character and conduct in the lover makes it not untrue to say that his world is indeed changed.

Social revolution, if it is real, is a change of that kind. The deeper the change, the more important the revolution; and very deep changes have, in fact, occurred in the past—but deeper may yet occur in the history of humanity. The outlook and attitude of all men in a large group may be made altogether different. The world, and still more our fellow-men, may be seen in an entirely new light. We may master our tradition and become creators of a new world.

Just such a change must occur if the worker's point of view is to become dominant in society. Nothing less will bring about the dissolution of the old society, whose structure is rigid with the admiration for wealth and rank and other idols of barbarism. But the real meaning of the idea of such a transformation may not be grasped. Mental or spiritual change is not easily understood ; and trivial instances of such change are too obvious for more important changes to be observed by the cursory glance which is all the practical man can afford to give to essentials. Thus even the French Revolution has been misunderstood. The mental transformation which at that time destroyed the power of privilege and "authority" in government is much less obvious, even after all these years, than the superficial change from monarchy to republic. So in our own case, we do not commonly grasp the character of intellectual or emotional revolution.

When a man's outlook is coloured by admiration for "superior" persons, his behaviour is different from what it is when his outlook is coloured by the expectation of greatness in any class and in any person. When a man's intellect is set in the direction of accepting and memorizing already acquired knowledge and habits, his daily acts are not what they would be if his intellect were set towards free speculation and adventurous ideas. To change from one such emotional or intellectual state to its opposite is to carry out a revolution. That transformation is not simply the acceptance of a new theory or the submission to waves of sudden emotionalism, as the gospellers of revolution seem to imagine. No revolution occurs when a man first learns of the atomic theory, nor when a man is first stirred by "jazz" music. The real revolution is a transformation of attitude and outlook, expressing itself in new kinds of action. The extreme example is "conversion" or falling in love: these may be revolutionary transformations of a personality, for to see and feel in a new way is a fairly common experience of individuals. In the same way there are group "conversions" when many men and women jointly change their attitude, as Florence did under the inspiration of Savonarola. Such transformations have occurred, for example, when Buddhism first spread in India or Christianity in the West, or at the Renaissance. These religious or intellectual revolutions are the most important changes in human history, which mark new beginnings; for what is characteristic of Christianity, for example, is not what it derived from the past, but what it substituted for the past. There are, indeed, better examples of social revolution in the history of religion than in political or economic history; and even in the history of the arts or sciences the transformations have been more radical than in politics.

Similarly, in the less fundamental issues of politics or economics, a revolution such as that in France at the close of the eighteenth century marked a new beginning, not because of the system of government set up, but because of the intellectual attitude and emotional allegiances which it established. Men stood upright in their own right then and devoted themselves to freedom and not to kings. But if a still greater revolution may yet be accomplished, it cannot be achieved by the emotional appeal of rhetoric, still less by the barbarism of abuse.

Turn now to consider what occurs in reform. The change is gradual, and each item, taken singly, appears to be trivial. The sight of a complicated draft law enrages the hot gospeller of revolution, because he cannot see the quality of the change implied. Simple minds require shocks in order to induce the belief that an event is occurring; and of course it is true that the forms of change may be used to disguise the fact that no real change is made. Even the establishment of a Republic may be a means for securing autocracy. But if reform is real, although it is gradual and limited, the effects are far-reaching. A mere extension of the hours of leisure may be the origin of a free economic society displacing economic slavery. The first use of reform is the treatment of superficial or subordinate ills, for these are not to be despised even if they will never prove mortal. A man's headache may be worth curing even if that leaves him still suffering from heartache. Small ills are real enough, and their cure in social policy is reform. Reformers are therefore never to be despised, and they should in any normal society be much more active and numerous than revolutionaries. But the second use of reform is preparatory: every step may be good or bad by reference to its direction, for change in the wrong direction may be worse than maintaining the old position. Reform, therefore, should lead towards great changes such as would, if they were sudden, be regarded as revolutionary.

Transformations in individual life as complete as that of conversion have been wrought by much less noticeable changes. The majority of those who develop into manhood out of childhood have done so by gradual and limited steps; and similarly the changes by which the industrial era replaced mediævalism were gradual, but the transformation has been complete. The speed with which a change is accomplished is of subordinate importance by comparison with its completeness and its security when it has been accomplished.

The real value of reform, then, is that it is a cause of revolution; and the test of a good revolution is that it can use the results and continue to use the methods of reform. A revolution not based upon the success of past reforms is insecure; for it may assume the existence of habits which have not yet become familiar even to the revolutionaries. On the other hand, reforms which do not lead towards a complete transformation of outlook and action are merely drugs for enduring evil. The reformer who is opposed to revolution is probably a reactionary in disguise. It follows that both reform and revolution are methods which may be useful for the treatment of different evils at different times or places; and we appear to have come now in the West to a point at which we need an "inner" mental change of attitude so fundamental as to be called revolutionary.

A new beginning cannot occur without a powerful will towards it dominating at least a small group in any community. A new world cannot be established by voting, nor by legislation, nor by economic reorganization, nor by dictatorial decree. All these are methods of reform. They cannot achieve a revolution. They can make men act differently for the same ends they had in view before or make them express differently the thoughts they inherited; but a real revolution occurs only when new ends are before us and new thoughts within. It is no revolution which transfers one man's million pounds so that a million men have one pound, if they all want to use their single pounds as the one man used his million; for the same uses will soon operate to transfer all those pounds again into the hands of one. There is no great harm in redistributing wealth. It may lead to better uses of wealth; but it may not. Our interest here is not the mere external change, but a transformation of outlook and action which will establish in power the worker's point of view; and this implies the dominance of an entirely new use of wealth and power.

All the tendencies and conceptions which have been discussed are preliminary, not final. They imply that a beginning, and not a conclusion, is to be made; for it is assumed that we are now at a stage of human development in which the future lies open to movement in a new direction. True—we are not without ancestors; for our fathers and grandfathers live in us still, as we shall survive in the passions and desires of our children. In that sense the new world is the natural development of the past and the present; but that is not its most important characteristic. One of the most obsolete assumptions of the older revolutionaries was that the new world they promised was a conclusion to a process. They were delighted to show that capitalism would pass from small-scale to large-scale organization, and so to State-socialism—as if that were the end and not the beginning of a tragic comedy. They suffered from the prevailing mythology of the nineteenth century, which vitiates the older Evolutionism—the mythology of the present as an end. They really believed that the process of evolution was excellent in so far as it led up to them and their ideas! They felt the long toil of humanity to be justified because it had produced the first chapter of their works. But that was long ago. We do not now think of ourselves as the end of evolution, nor do we imagine that our conceptions are final, for we know that the most important characteristic of our desires and our ideals is not that we know where they came from, but that we do *not* know where they will end. We are sure of ourselves, not because we are sons of our fathers, but because we are fathers of our sons; and we are therefore confident, not that the present is wicked, but that the future will be better. We cannot, therefore, offer our conceptions as conclusions to be accepted; we suggest them only as hypotheses to be used as a first vintage. We know in what direction we are moving, but we do not know our goal. We do not know the exact form of the society which will eliminate the evils of poverty, oppression and war; but we know that it will not be less civilized or less interesting or less varied than society to-day.

Men with more bread available will not want less music. Men in good houses will not want less learning or less companionship. Of course those who are well satisfied already tend to think of a demand for bread as materialistic or degrading. Bread to a full man is mere matter; but bread to an empty man is part of his blood and his spirit. So when we demand bread for the starving we are seeking, not for possession, but for spiritual life; and when we discuss freedom we are seeking, not for release from social life, but for power to increase it. That all this should come without confusion will be dependent upon our skill in the social arts; for it requires a finer contact between persons than is now common to make the change run smoothly. In Western countries we may not be yet civilized enough to achieve a real revolution. We still prefer to hit a man on the head rather than meet him in fair argument. But in China there is a book on the Art of War, written in the sixth century before Christ, which says: "The greatest general is he who wins a victory without fighting a battle." So the real revolution must be without confusion.

All those transformations which we envisage can take place without injury, perhaps even with positive advantage, to the best that we have inherited from the past. Of course some who have possessions will have to lose them; but that is no injury even to them. Some think a good motor might as well not exist as belong to someone else. What is not theirs is worse than nothing. But that is the attitude of the barbarian; for the civilized men the fact that a picture is admired by Smith is more important than that it is owned by Jones. That motor-cars and trains exist is important, but it is quite unimportant to civilization that the present few should be able to use them. We look forward, then, to the general acceptance of the belief that ownership is irrelevant. The use of all that is best would not then be less excellent than it now is.

It is sometimes imagined that those who have nothing to lose, having no possessions and no power, will not be able to control themselves if wealth be more freely distributed. But we are too confident of the sanity and kindliness of common men to fear for the best that is in the world. The achievements of the past are not likely to perish through the desires of the many although they may be endangered by the selfishness of the few. A great change may yet come without noise and confusion. Security and confidence must be the greater part of our strength. We shall be tempted to crude hates and violent anger. But we know that no great deed can be accomplished except in quiet, and that the only possible basis for freedom is the prevalence of peace.

It must not, however, be assumed that the transformation is indefinitely postponed. The danger in the conception of a peaceful change is that the more important part of it may seem to be its peacefulness and not the fact that it is a change. Thus many reformers are misled into devoting all their energy to details, and the life goes out of the determination that fundamental evils shall be destroyed. For that reason we must insist upon the immediate possibility of a real revolution. The right moment may not have come; but it is near. Men now living will see the transformation. The will makes itself felt: the Titan is stirring. The future does not include only gradual and limited reforms; for indeed the accumulation of past reforms has already made the continuance of minor adjustments a matter of subordinate importance. Of course it is necessary, as any worker knows, to glance at the ground under your feet when you are passing through the sheds; but the time comes when you must lift up your eyes to control the machine. So in our own lifetime we shall put our hands upon the force that moves the world. That will be the real social transformation. It will be lucky for the professed revolutionaries if they know it for what it is, when it comes; for those who expect a Messiah do not always recognize him when he appears. The main issue, however, is that the transformation shall occur, and that soon.

The general change in the dominant attitude of men will involve the establishment of work as the sole ground of honour and the only source of power or rights; and work means nothing mysterious, but the ordinary acts of dustmen, engine-drivers and miners. As it has been shown, there is no fundamental difference between the various forms of human energy, whether they produce bread and boots or pictures and poetry. But there is an important difference between the exercise of energy and the control of its products, wealth and accumulated power, if this control is for the sake of private ease and enjoyment. In our day the private control of wealth and the absorption by a few of the finer results of civilization are thought honourable, but work is regarded as despicable or, at the best, as a necessary evil. That, however, is a transitory superstition supporting a primitive custom; and the civilization which results is trivial. The honour of the man who works, nevertheless, already begins to be felt by some workers; and when that true sense of honour displaces more barbaric admirations those who work will have strength to live a fuller and a nobler life.

INDEX